peckish

ALSO BY
SUZANNE LENZER

Graze

Truly Madly Pizza

peckish

Suggestions for the Sophisticated Snacker

SUZANNE LENZER

PHOTOGRAPHY BY KATE S. JORDAN

RODALE
NEW YORK

Published in the United States by Rodale Books, an imprint of Random House,
a division of Penguin Random House LLC, New York.

Rodale & Plant with colophon is a registered trademark of Penguin Random
House LLC.

Library of Congress Cataloging-in-Publication Data
Names: Lenzer, Suzanne, author.
Title: Peckish / Suzanne Lenzer.
Description: First edition. | New York, NY: Rodale, [2025] | Includes index.
Identifiers: LCCN 2024012598 (print) | LCCN 2024012599 (ebook) |
    ISBN 9780593797006 (hardcover) | ISBN 9780593797013 (ebook)
Subjects: LCSH: Snack foods. | Appetizers. | LCGFT: Cookbooks.
Classification: LCC TX740 .L46 2025 (print) | LCC TX740 (ebook) |
    DDC 641.5/3—dc23/eng/20240410
LC record available at https://lccn.loc.gov/2024012598
LC ebook record available at https://lccn.loc.gov/2024012599

Printed in China

RodaleBooks.com | RandomHouseBooks.com

9 8 7 6 5 4 3 2 1

First Edition

Book design by Rae Ann Spitzenberger
Prop Styling by Christina Lane

My Gruyère cheese puffs
straight from the oven
say I'm glad you're here.
Sit down, relax. I'll look
after everything.

—ANN PATCHETT

Potted Salmon, Smoked and Fresh (page 85);
Jammy Eggs with Fried Shallots (page 113);
and Carta di Musica (page 192)

CONTENTS

SOPHISTICATED SNACKING, DEFINED

Since before I was old enough to actually cook, I was besotted with a fantasy of my grown-up life, one that would include throwing elaborate dinner parties in candlelit rooms, endless lunches on pretty plaid blankets by the sea, and long, leisurely breakfasts on terraces that were yet to be revealed to me. As a teenager, when the *Los Angeles Times Magazine* would show up at our house on Sundays, I'd flip straight to the food column to see which dishes sounded worthy of my mental menus. Then when the *Martha Stewart Living* magazine and *Lee Bailey's Country Weekends* came on the scene, they beckoned with their glossy photos of elegant parlor parties and dreamy lakeside soirees, and I was further smitten.

I wanted to conceive and create with the same fabulousness that I saw in their pages. There would be multiple courses with silverware to suit and dishes with names like coq au vin and cassoulet. I would make flawless appetizers and all-day braises, rustic salads and long-simmering stews; I would dazzle with cobblers, crisps, tarts, and tortes. Such was my teenage idea of sophisticated cooking and entertaining, and it has taken years to let go of these heady visions. Only now, as a recovering overachiever at the stove, can I say how freeing it is to let go of this idea that food must be hard fought and overwrought to be wonderful. It needn't.

I still find the process of curating and creating an extravagant meal enchanting, but it's ultimately sharing the end product of all that labor with the people I care about that counts. That's what we cooks thrive on. At our core, I do believe that most cooks, even those who love the process deeply, want to be loved for our food. We share it as an act of devotion, and what we hope for in return—the accolades, the satisfied bellies—are equally as satiating to us as the meal may be to our friends or family. "Here is my heart," we say. "Bon appétit."

And while the creation of these ideal meals is rewarding, the hard truth is that it's also draining. As calming as my time in the kitchen may be when I'm lost in kneading bread or stirring risotto, entertaining can be more frenetic than zen. By the time I've done the work and sometimes have redone it, I too am kind of, well, done. Consider the tart crust: "Yes, I thought adding ground pecans to the pastry would be just right for the lemon sabayon, but it's actually nuttier than I'd hoped, so just give me a half hour to make another batch." Or this one: "Yes, I know we don't need both pâté and rillettes for appetizers, but it just feels more, well, *more.* Please go get the chicken livers . . . oh, and some fresh raspberries if they look nice?"

We all know the saying about how it's the journey and not the destination, but when it comes to entertaining, it's equally about both. The act of cooking offers its own soul-soothing benefits, but when we try too hard, we can easily lose sight of what all the work is really about: not culinary acrobatics to rival restaurant fare, not worrying about the sauce curdling or the chicken charring, and certainly not fretting about whether it's Instagram worthy, but being where we want to be—sipping and snacking with the people we love.

It's taken me way too long to figure out that my favorite food experiences are often over the kitchen counter or standing midway between the sink and the stove, so caught up in the conversation at hand that simmering pots are neglected and salad dressings are left half-made. What's come to me at last is that many of the most compelling discussions and deepest fits of laughter happen in between the making and the meal itself. These moments are perfect because they have all the features one hopes for in the feast without the organization, orchestration, and yes, exhaustion. So why not liberate ourselves and embrace the truth? So often it's the snacks, the tastes in between, that make our hearts race. And they too can be sophisticated, I assure you.

It's the Snacks That Get Me

Over the years, what I cook and eat has changed. Even how I cook and eat has altered. Some of this is likely the natural result of cooking for a living. As I spend so much time and energy thinking about food for others, when it comes to cooking at home, I'm guilty of giving in to routine and laziness. But I've come to see this as a gift; I can throw dinner together thoughtfully but without too much heavy lifting (mental or physical). Yet there's more to it than just giving in to what is simple to make; it's also that these days I choose to eat in a simpler fashion. What I crave is food that's blatantly unfussy and only lightly touched but still varied and a bit peripatetic.

Today I'm drawn to small dishes, but instead of forming full meals around them, I'm happy to surrender to a more free-form, wandering sensibility, to indulge in the pleasure of being a culinary vagabond. A small plate of crispy favas with fried parsley makes me happy, as does a more robust platter of fig panzanella, the bread soaked and softened by a bright vinaigrette. A slice of tortilla—slivered potatoes nestled between custardy egg and a bit of shrimp and jamón—nibbled over the counter when it's just about five o'clock and there's a glass of white wine to be had is often all it takes to make me feel the world is steady.

These are my favorite food events, what I refer to as the "in-between meals." The snacks shared standing over the stove with a tipple in hand, during that hour so commonly called "happy," when I'm gathered at the kitchen island with friends and a smattering of random bites. It's the snacks that get me. And often it's their haphazard nature that's so seductive. Yes, snacking is my meal of choice. It can be one dish or ten, it can be a collection of toasts or a platter of greens and a jar of pickles. No matter the curation, it's when we all seem most relaxed, when the food is less choreographed and the experience is more authentic. There doesn't need to be a strict menu or sensibility to it, rather simply an array of delicious flavors set out in a thoughtful manner.

Vanilla-Lemon Posset with Stone Fruit Compote (page 227); Chocolate Pots with Boozy Cream (page 224); and Almond and Orange Lace Sandwich Cookies (page 218)

Sardine Rillettes with Avocado and Fennel (page 53)

Letting Go, Being Bold, Becoming Peckish

A few years ago, as time became somewhat blurry and routines lost their structure, as we all found ourselves more prone to a cloistered existence, my life in the kitchen was rejiggered as well. There was more time to play and less reason to worry about efforts gone awry. Some days I had less energy, so I gave in to trying new shortcuts, which often yielded wondrous results (some stumbled miserably, but at least I'd relinquished that fear of failure for a moment). Then, as life became more familiar again, as friends came back into the fold, there was a new spontaneity to how we gathered, and this impacted how I made, served, and shared food as well. Welcoming unexpected freedom, unintended bravery, and frankly some chaos into my kitchen felt perfectly natural considering how unnatural everything else felt. It was invigorating. Enlivening in fact. And this is what I hope this book will do for you—give you permission to experience freedom, bravery, and a sense of wild abandon in your kitchen too.

Rest assured: Thoughtful snacking is not complicated and does not require long days spent at the stove. While it does require a modicum of planning, the benefits exponentially outweigh the effort. To wit, once you've made a jar of pickles or a pot of pâté, they are there in the fridge for days for your snacking pleasure. Freeze an unbaked batch of gougères so anytime a friend swings by you can pop them in the oven for a fresh treat; the same goes for tater tots. Marinate baby artichokes or beans and not only do you have something to nibble, but they can be happily tossed in salads or pasta, smeared on toasts, or scattered on pizzas.

And, while all these "tastes" can be made to stand alone, they are also ripe for pairing in whimsical and, yes, random ways. None of these dishes are hard, and many rely simply on pantry staples and a few fresh ingredients. Because every recipe is on the easy end of the cooking spectrum (some are truly more about assemblage than actual cooking), you can get lost in the flavors and the eating experience itself, rather than complex techniques or an excessive time commitment.

THE SNACKER'S PANTRY
AND OTHER THOUGHTS

I Could Probably Live on Bread Alone

I have become resigned to accommodating the various eating restrictions
(or foibles) that seem to be so common these days. Vegetarian feasts are not
a problem, and I'm pretty good at making a dairy-free meal that isn't reliant
on jackfruit or nutritional yeast to feel complete. If you're doing the hunter-
gatherer thing this week, just let me know ahead of time (so I can hunt and
gather). However, if you announce that you've joined the gluten-free craze
and want me to indulge this trend, you will hear me sigh audibly with deep
disappointment. Certainly, I understand if you have Celiac disease or some
other health-related issue, but if you're just ditching bread for the sake of
vanity, because you've been told it will make your skin glow and your brain
defog, I beg you to reconsider.

Bread—and by that, I mean good quality, minimal ingredients—is one
of the eater's great joys. The heel of a baguette, a nub of sourdough, a hunk
of focaccia, a slice of brioche or a flatbread—each offers the basis for so many
different and exciting adventures when it comes to what to eat that it's hard
to overstate the importance it plays in my kitchen. In fact, bread is often the
basis for where I begin planning what to make; it has a gravitational pull,
a magnetic ability to attract flavors and ingredients, making it the perfect
place to begin. It can be as simple as salty butter and a slice of tomato on
toast or more involved like a charred cube of olive oil–soaked ciabatta
skewered with figs and Stilton cheese; regardless, bread is foundational in a
way that few other ingredients are.

And here's the thing: Bread is about more than physical sustenance.
Like tending a garden, bread baking offers the opportunity for mental and
emotional meditation. If you're even a little bit inclined, baking your own
bread, even low-lifts like focaccia or a simple flatbread, are the kind of

kitchen soul-craft that comes close to transcendent. You may struggle at times, you may have some fails, but the process of learning and the elation when you succeed will leave you giddy, I promise.

And what's more, sharing a loaf of bread you've made yourself with friends will always leave you glowing (far more than eliminating it from your diet, contrary to what you might have heard). The gratitude and awe people show when it comes to homemade bread never ceases to amaze me. During our pandemic time, homemade bread making became an international fetish of sorts, a sliver of light during that bewildering era. And while some people have latched onto it as part of their postpandemic routine, sadly many seem to have left their starters to languish in the back of the fridge. This is a shame, because making your own bread can make you a happier person and make the people you care about happier too. But if you don't have the time or the desire to tackle baking, that's okay—just pledge to buy the good stuff.

Fruit and Vegetables with a Side of Honesty

Unless you live in California, Italy, Mexico, or other gorgeous places where the sun shines a large part of the year and agriculture is a vibrant part of the culture, you simply cannot eat seasonally and locally all year long unless you are content to subsist on root vegetables. And I am not. I love potatoes, parsnips, leeks, carrots, beets, and celeriac too—dearly, in fact, but I need more. Which is where the honesty comes in: I buy avocados all year long, make salad from lettuces grown on the other coast, and rely on citrus that most certainly took a long trip to find its way to my kitchen (often it appears in a flat-rate box from my mom's garden in Los Angeles or the Berkeley yard of my editor, Dervla, so I know exactly how many air miles it has racked up). I try, but eating locally and seasonally on the East Coast is a limited time opportunity, and while I embrace it during the months when it's feasible, much of the year I'm forced to buy food from farther afield. And I'm okay with that.

I completely understand that we shouldn't be eating stone fruit in December and that English peas are really at their best only in spring, but as someone who loves to cook and eat, I've had to embrace some inconvenient truths about my habits and in turn have devised some workarounds that keep me feeling both satiated and conscientious.

First, I have no issue with frozen vegetables. I don't think they're all equal, and I don't bother with many of them (fresh carrots are easy enough to come by, so frozen are not better or easier, really), but I find frozen peas are often just as flavorful as fresh and they certainly tend to be more consistent. While they're in season I will always buy fresh (the shelling alone is worth it), but you'll never find my freezer devoid of a bag because they are absurdly useful in pastas, toast toppings, soups, stews, and, in a pinch, a chopped salad.

A box of frozen spinach is actually better than fresh in stuffed pastas, as fresh cooks down to so little that you need masses to make up what you get in a box. Frozen peaches and cherries will never make as good a pie as those you find at a farmstand in July, but if you're craving a crumble or crisp with something other than apples or pears in midwinter, they'll scratch that itch. And if you want to feel really clever, freeze bags of washed and pitted stone fruit or any kind of berries during the summer and then have them on hand during the darker days. I try to keep them separated, but when the fruit starts to go soft, I often end up with mixed tubs of blueberries, blackberries, strawberries, and raspberries, meaning my winter tarts are nearly always of the mixed-berry variety.

I also do have a few hall passes when it comes to off-season fruit and vegetables. As I mentioned, there's avocados; I can't live without them, so they are grandfathered in as acceptable all year round. Tomatoes fall into this category too, although here I am rather finicky. The tomatoes we get here on the East Coast in summer are so absolutely stunningly delicious that I eat my weight in them while I can. At the same time, I freeze ziplock bags of fresh plum tomatoes to have on hand during winter for those certain sauces that benefit from fresh over canned (though I adore canned tomatoes too). And then in winter I tend to buy cherry tomatoes and Campari tomatoes, the smaller varieties that seem to have more flavor than the larger ones when grown in greenhouses. No, they don't compare with August's bounty, but tomatoes are essential for me, so spending a bit more and seeking out edible ones off-season is rationalized.

All that said, I avoid asparagus in winter, and the same goes for summer squash and corn and anything that really suffers when it's not peak-of-season fresh. But that just means that hearty greens like broccoli rabe, kale, and chard are more important. I buy a head of romanesco any time I see one, and acorn or Delicata squash too. These are the compromises that I can live with; everyone has to find the balance that works best for their conscience, their budget, and their taste buds. With all that in mind, here's my advice: Come spring, indulge in asparagus like it's going out of style, and in summer, eat a tomato or a peach every chance you get. Then take solace in potatoes.

Charcuterie and Cheese, My Love Language

Give me a slice of soppressata and a hunk of Manchego any day over a molten chocolate cake or a lighter-than-air mousse. Some people covet sweets, but my DNA is definitely partial to savory and, more specifically, cheeses and cured meats. What both of these food groups offer that I find so hard to resist is variation. There are seemingly endless cheeses to try on this planet, and many more cured meats than I'll ever be able to enjoy. And here's a wonderful truth: Learning a bit about the different kinds of cheeses and meats out there makes experimenting much more fun. As someone who has admitted (in print!) to being ever so intimidated by the all-knowing cheesemonger and humbled before the artisanal charcuterie counter, I feel better armed with a bit of knowledge when I shop.

So here are the two key bits of high-level cheese knowledge that I find helpful in navigating the evermore exciting cheese counter. First, there are families of cheese (think fresh, bloomy rind, washed rind, pressed, blue, and so on), each with their own appearance, aroma, flavor, and texture. As I understand it, there is no set number of families, though, and different mongers may define cheeses differently. However, understanding the variation can help you know what you're looking at and tasting. What is definable, though, are the different types of milk (cow, sheep, and goat) that cheese is made from. And knowing the different milks can help you understand more about what kinds of cheese you gravitate toward.

Second, and this is something I've found incredibly helpful: European cheeses offer up a wide array of eating experiences while American-crafted cheeses are much more discrete. In other words, if you enjoyed a Comté or a Cantal, you've had a regional style cheese that is just one of many that goes by the same name. And each will vary in flavor, depending on myriad factors, from what the farmers feed their animals to the unique process of each producer. In contrast, American cheesemakers identify their cheeses both by their own names as well as the specific cheese name. So if you've fallen hard for Vermont Creamery's Cremont or Consider Bardwell's Pawlet, you can reliably assume it will be the same cheese every time you buy it.

I like to think of cheese like perfume; what works for one person may not for the next. To learn what works for you, taste as much as you can and make notes about which styles and producers you love. Finding new cheeses to love is exciting, but it's important to have old familiars that you can confidently keep in the fridge at all times too.

The same is true when it comes to charcuterie. It's easy to fall back on prosciutto di Parma and sweet soppressata time and again, but being a little daring at the deli counter will be hugely rewarding. And while American grocery stores have upped their cheese game immensely, many of these cheese counters are so well stocked with prepackaged options, it's hard to ask for tastes. Delicatessens, on the other hand, tend to be more accommodating with samples. If you want to try speck (a smoky cured ham from the north of Italy) or bresaola (a lean cured beef with a nutty, sweet flavor), there's no harm in asking for a sliver before committing to a full quarter pound. And if you're really intrigued and want to reach beyond coppa and finocchiona, seek out Varzi and lonza, give 'nduja—a spreadable sausage made with Calabrian chiles—a try on toast, or splash out on a few slices of different salumi and other cured hams just for the sake of exploration. And ask questions; in my experience a good butcher or deli associate will know enough to help guide you if you're bold enough to engage in a conversation. Like cheese (and anything, really), to know if you like it, you have to try it.

Happiness Is a Good Grocery Store

Some people brag about living near the water. Some rave about being able to walk into town for a coffee. For years I was spoiled by a wealth of incredible food shopping. Before we moved to Connecticut, I lived in a corner of New York City that was within walking distance of Bleecker Street (the location of my favorite butcher, Italian deli, and a world-famous cheese shop); Chelsea Market (a destination for incredible fish, another great cheese shop, an artisanal butcher, and a litany of other small food purveyors); Union Square Greenmarket; and Eataly (an Italian food emporium). If I felt like really getting in my exercise, I could wander up to some amazing Middle Eastern shops in Midtown or meander south to the awe-inspiring experience that is Chinatown. All that, plus a very solid local market for the basics right on the corner (oh, and they delivered). This was a remarkable quirk of real estate, my bounty of shopping choices, but from a work perspective as a food stylist, it was also wildly convenient; I could do all my shopping simply by cleverly mapping out my morning.

I no longer have the convenience that the city offers, as we've become solidly suburban dwellers. Still, I count myself very lucky. I have a local market where I shop for 90 percent of my groceries. I've also found a small fruit and vegetable shop that carries some lovely local produce, and there's a good butcher shop nearby. A few towns over are some fantastic Hispanic and Asian markets, and if all else fails and I really need something specific, online is always an option. My point is twofold: I am still very lucky, but more importantly, exciting food shopping doesn't require you to live in a major city and you don't have to rely on a slew of rarefied gourmet shops to make great food. I like food shopping (while some people head for the museum or the cathedral when they travel, you'll find me at the farmers' market), but I do not think food should be so precious that you have to hit three stores to make a meal. I like to, but you may not, and that's totally okay. The recipes in this book were all made from ingredients I buy regularly— little here is fancy and it's all right out of my pantry or off the shelves of my local shops.

And while I don't want anyone going out and shopping for things they may never use (it makes me crazy when a recipe calls for half a teaspoon of nigella seeds that I'll use once and then throw out five years later when I discover them at the back of the spice drawer), keeping a well-stocked pantry is practical. With that in mind, here's a peek into the pantry that the ideas in this book come from, a glimpse into the jars, tins, bags, and boxes of stuff I keep on hand, as well as thoughts on the produce and other fresh ingredients I use with enough regularity that, while they live in the fridge, to me they count as pantry basics.

PANTRY MUST-HAVES

Extra-virgin olive oil

Red wine vinegar

Sherry vinegar

Fine sea salt

Maldon sea salt (flake)

Peppercorns

Harissa

Dijon mustard

Country-style Dijon mustard

Ketchup

Hot sauce (green and red)

Toasted sesame oil

Soy sauce

Ponzu

Rice wine vinegar

Old Bay

Smoked pimentón

Cumin

Fennel seeds

Red pepper flakes

Dried whole red chiles

ESSENTIAL SNACKING INGREDIENTS

Italian-style tuna (in olive oil)

Sardines

Anchovies

Smoked salmon and/or trout

Olives

Canned beans (butter beans, cannellini, black beans, and chickpeas)

Dry beans (chickpeas, favas)

Nuts (almonds, pecans, walnuts, pistachios)

Cornichons

Canned tomatoes

Canned artichoke hearts

Pasta (long and cut)

Kasha, farro, and rice

Capers

FRESH STUFF TO HAVE ON HAND

Lemons

Limes

Crunchy vegetables (cucumbers, radish, fennel, etc.)

Cheese

Charcuterie

Parmesan

Eggs

Salted butter

Unsalted butter

Milk

Greek yogurt

Ricotta cheese

Crème fraîche or clotted cream

BAKING NECESSITIES

Bread flour

All-purpose flour

"00" flour

Semolina flour

Almond flour

Polenta

Potato starch

Active dry yeast

Sugar

Demerara sugar

Vanilla beans

Cocoa

Chocolate chips

Chocolate (60% and 70% cacao)

A Short Diatribe on Growing Things

I wasn't born a gardener, but I've definitely grown into one. To me it's like being a runner; you don't have to be great at it, you just have to love it. I may run a slow and sloppy ten-minute mile, and I may lapse from my daily laps now and again, but no matter, if you ask me, I'm a runner because it's part of my identity. The same goes for gardening. My plot may look a bit more Miss Havisham than Martha Stewart, but in my bones, I'm a gardener. I grow things (and sometimes, instead, I inadvertently kill them), and while I'm taken with trees and smitten with shrubs, it's vegetables, fruits, and herbs galore that really get me.

My first experience with growing things was in the small beach town of Milford, Connecticut, when Ken's job took us out of the city for a year. The house we rented for our *Green Acres* adventure (if you're unfamiliar, it's a sitcom starring Eva Gabor about a banker and his wife who leave the city to become farmers) was hardly on par with the pristine corporate apartment that was being proffered up by his company, but it was perfect for us: An old Cape on the water with a wildly overgrown but fenced-in vegetable patch and a mature asparagus bed that had been left to languish in the weeds. The owner said we could do what we liked with the yard, and so, with the blind enthusiasm (and utter ignorance) of freshly minted suburbanites, we set about making a garden. The short version of this is that while ramshackle in appearance and uneven in terms of success, we both fell hard for digging in the dirt.

Today we have a new garden—well, a very old and neglected garden we are trying to revitalize—one that continues to teach us a hundred lessons every season. With gardening you can really only get smarter, and here's a tip if you're reading this and under forty (okay, fifty): Start gardening now, fall in love with plants and planting today, because gardens take time to become what you hope they'll be, years in fact. Plus, you'll make mistakes that take more than a season to set right (it's sad but true). Older gardeners may have the wisdom, but younger gardeners have time on their side—and the more time you have in your garden, the happier you'll be.

Here's another tip: If you want to be a vegetable gardener (and if you cook, this is definitely what you want to be), then the first thing to do when you get a little patch of dirt in the sun is to plant an asparagus bed. Asparagus roots take three to four years to become productive givers, and if you spend even one year noodling on it instead of going for it, that's one more year of not having those glorious green spears welcome you to the start of spring. The same goes for fruit trees—sooner is better. And while

you're at it, plant some rhubarb and strawberries too—fruit and vegetables that come back year after year are simply the best. That said, if you don't have the luxury yet of a small bit of land, don't be deterred: You'll do fine with some pots on a fire escape, a box in the window, or even a little tray of herbs on the countertop.

Growing things and being a cook are intertwined in my mind. Both are crafts that demand some basic following of directions and ideally, some natural instinct (though this last bit can be overcome with enough commitment and some good teachers). Both also benefit from a sense of bravery and resilience in the face of failure, which most cooks I know have in spades. However, even if you have no interest in full-fledged gardening, if you like to cook you will never regret keeping a small forest of culinary herbs nearby—basil, rosemary, flat-leaf parsley, oregano, thyme, cilantro, and a few chives are a good start. No matter how small, snipping a few leaves off your own living plant will always feel (and taste) better than pulling a plastic bag or box out of the fridge and trying to salvage those few perky leaves from the sad, wilted ones.

The Joy of Solo Snacking

Cookbooks are, generally speaking, geared toward cooking for others and communal eating experiences, whether that's a late-morning slice of cake with a neighbor, a meandering lunch with family, dinner with your partner, or a holiday feast with a few friends. And this one is no exception; I want you to make these different recipes to share with others. But I'd be remiss if I didn't say that some of my favorite meals have happened in solitude and that part of what I love most about the style of eating I advocate for in this collection is that it's perfect for one. Snacking is, by its nature, the way many of us eat when we're solo, whether that's smashing half an avocado on a piece of toast for lunch or something wholly more involved.

To me the notion of a bowl of cereal eaten, halfheartedly, standing over the sink has always been a sad one, not least because it implies an intrinsic loss of ceremony, a lack of thoughtfulness around food eaten when there's no one to share it with. It suggests that when we're left to eat by ourselves it's just about physical sustenance and not about emotional nourishment, the kind we expect to gain from our shared food experiences. And as for ease, smart snacking often demands no more effort than that bowl of cereal.

The loneliness suggested by the blindly consumed bowl of cereal is real, but the idea that this is what solitary eating is or should be is ridiculous.

*Tangy Lemon Tartlets
(page 228)*

Eating alone, if given the attention it deserves, is not just a satisfying experience but an act of self-empowerment. How often do you get to eat just what you want without conferring with others or asking the proverbial question "What do you want for dinner?" How freeing is it to open the fridge and pull out a few random bits that suit your mood without wondering if the combination will fall flat for someone else, without doing the mental gymnastics necessary to figure out how to make more than just you happy? Of course it's warming to satisfy others, but it's equally rewarding to treat ourselves, even when we're by ourselves, to that level of happiness as well.

When I make food with the same energy and care for myself that I would if someone else was joining me at the table, the meal becomes akin to a meditation; rather than rushing through for sustenance, I find myself relishing the quiet and the space to really taste each bite, to truly savor my choices. Far from finding a solo meal lonely, I tend to find it liberating. And snacking, or at least snacking on the food such as you'll find here, is perfect for this kind of satiation. A toast and a small platter of veggies, a hunk of bread dipped into a jar of this or a dish of that—these are the kinds of things that are ideal for eating on your own.

One of my favorite solo meals can loosely be called a salad: It's a rather heaping bowl of baby arugula doused in olive oil and lemon juice and topped with paper-thin slices of fennel, half a sliced avocado laid next to some jarred Italian tuna, a jammy egg snuggled alongside, if I have one, and a few slices of cucumber and a couple of handfuls of potato chips to finish it all off (for the recipe, see page 172). This is less a recipe and more a mash-up of some of my favorite things, but more than that, it is a meal made exactly the way I like it. No one to say arugula is too spicy, no one asking me to hold the egg, and no one raising an eyebrow at that second handful of chips. It's pure delight because it's exactly what I like and how I like it.

Eating with friends and family—and of course cooking for people—is a joy. But so is doing it simply for yourself. Bringing the same ceremony to eating alone that you do to sharing is a way of treating yourself thoughtfully, not to mention deliciously.

On Drinking (or Not)

A glass of wine, sometimes two, at the end of the day is one of the things I enjoy most in this world. Yet even in writing it down, I feel a bit uneasy, a tad guilty, declaring that. Alcohol, like food, has become a loaded subject in our current culture: Are we drinking too much and more than our friends? Are we oddly proud when we take a break to "dry out"? And why has something that confers such pleasure become associated with "self-medicating"? I think about all this, and then I think, damn, I wish I were French. A Frenchwoman probably wouldn't get herself all twisted up over her relationship with a glass of Pouilly Fume. It all seems to have become so complicated.

But the reality, for me, is this: A glass or two of wine or a beer, or the odd cocktail when I'm feeling like something more decadent, is totally okay. As is taking a break now and then to reset. How and what we drink are personal choices, just like what we eat. Moderation is the sweet spot for me, and I've decided to be good with that. I am very fond of wine, and I like sharing a bottle with friends as much as I sometimes cherish a quiet glass on my own. In fact, while drinking alone as a concept carries its own baggage, it's something I also take deep pleasure in doing. A quiet night alone with a plate of snacks and a beer is relaxing. And even better, after a long day of work, it's hard to overstate how nice it is to indulge in what we, in our house, call "shower wine." A glass to sip while you rinse off the remains of the day and change into softer clothes is a lovely way to transition from the world outside to the safety and calm of home. If you do drink, I highly recommend trying it.

In terms of what I drink, and how I pair those choices with food, well, that's all rather random. Some people are very serious about their pairings, but I tend to simply follow the "drink what you like" approach. Which is why the rules of what color goes with which food or season or temperature don't apply in our house; it's really about what suits our mutual palate and mood. More often than not, what we drink is not extravagant. We have house wines that we buy by the case—affordable, solid choices that we know and can open reliably. And while we are hardly collectors, we also keep a few special wines on hand: Bottles that we know and love, new ones that just called out from the shelf wanting to be tried, ones we break out when there's a special occasion or a hankering for something a little fancy.

Deciding what to drink (or what to serve when you entertain) comes with knowing your own taste, feeling confident in your choices, and not being cowed into buying more expensive wines or esoteric liquors simply because you think you should. I've found that getting to know the merchants at our local wine store is immensely helpful; not only do they know their stock and are usually thrilled to chat about what they like, but over time they've grown to know what I like as well, so they can readily recommend new things with a sense of what I want. In my experience, while there will be wine snobs who will intimidate ("wine-speak," as my friend Erica calls it, can be tedious), most of the people working in wine and beer these days, and booze in general, are just excited about the industry and happy to share their knowledge. So, like cooking itself, summoning some bravery to ask questions and take (affordable) chances is worthwhile when it comes to enjoying drinking. And, if you're not drinking, dabbling in some of the newer nonalcoholic beers and other beverages can be fun too.

PARLOR TRICKS FOR SPONTANEOUS SNACKING

A Few Small Dishes of Crunchy, Salty, Briny Bits and Pieces

Based on the fact that I'm writing a book about food, you might mistakenly believe that I am one of those enviable people who regularly serves dinner for ten with no more than an hour's notice. As I said, you would be mistaken. I am actually someone who is better suited to having two or three people over for drinks and snacks without a second thought. That's because of the small-dish trick that I've successfully employed since college, back when my dinnerware was a mishmash of chipped hand-me-downs and garage sale finds, and my budget was whatever tips I'd made working as a barista. (It's worth noting, many of my favorite dishes are still of garage sale pedigree.)

Back then, having friends over meant sitting around an old trunk on a scratchy, secondhand couch I had inexpertly covered with a dark green sheet, while drinking white Zin or Amstel Light. It was *not* the height of elegance. However, my snacks were worth showing up for, not solely for what they were but also for how they were presented: A few beverage-friendly bites assembled on a mix of teacup saucers and other small Fiesta dinnerware side plates from the flea market. In college, this was what passed for thoughtful entertaining, as the glasses were made out of glass and the plates weren't paper. But it all happened utterly by accident: I would invite friends over, spur of the moment, and then realize I didn't have enough of any one or two things on hand to put out to eat. And while friends could be relied on to pick up a bottle or a six-pack on their way over, it was definitely on me, the host, to bring the snacks.

The first time this happened, I was saved by popcorn: one quick batch flavored three different ways, Old Bay being the favorite as I recall. When it became a pattern—enthusiastic invitations followed by the realization that I lacked all forethought in terms of food shopping—I made it part of my repertoire. "I'll just rustle something up" took on a very literal meaning when you came to my house, and while the fare is definitely better now, the concept is as unchanged as the outcome: happy snackers.

Aim for three or four (five if you're inspired, but any more and it becomes cluttered) small plates or bowls or a combination. And I do mean small, these are tiny dishes that make the food you're going to put on them look special. It may sound meager, and I can't explain the psychology behind it, but in my experience, people love to have a curated selection of bits and pieces to pick at, and when it's presented as less rather than more, the rarity is appealing. It also somehow implies that you thought seriously about what you're serving; you didn't just toss a bag of pretzels into a bowl or put some crackers on a plate with a piece of block cheese. No, you identified a few different ingredients and carefully plated them in a way that feels both intentional and well planned, an "I made this just for you" moment. (You and I may know you were a bit harried and in turn, hurried, but no one else need be the wiser.)

My go-to combinations today are a mix of fried fava beans, Marcona almonds, taralli, cubes or disks of salami, similarly cut semihard or hard cheese, olives, cornichons, artichoke hearts, pepperoncini, or anything briny and tangy, and sometimes, not always, a crunchy fresh vegetable if I have it (radish, cucumber, fennel, or the like) or a tender small fruit (figs, cherries, cherry plums, and grapes are nice). These are hardly the most exotic bites, but they work together well, and as I said, I always have just enough on hand to fill a small dish in a pinch. Certainly, you can throw in some slightly more quotidian ingredients as well (who doesn't love a Goldfish cracker or some spiced popcorn?), but the vaguely Mediterranean array I lean on is companionable, and as this is a back-pocket trick, the whole idea is to keep it easy. A few small dishes, enough of whatever you have in the pantry, and a full glass. Ta-dah.

The Bread and Spread Affair

I've long believed that you can gauge a restaurant by its bread basket, and I think the same holds true for the home cook. If you buy (or better yet, make) great bread, you're already ahead of the game. As I said earlier, bread is a key part of the snacker's pantry and having a good loaf, a stack of flatbreads, or a slab of focaccia on hand at all times can save you in myriad ways. I keep my homemade breads frozen so I can pull any of them out of the freezer as

*Artichoke and Green Olive Tapenade
(page 120); Arugula, White Bean,
and Roasted Garlic Smear (page 121);
and Fennel Ratatouille Salsa (page 124)*

Potted Salmon, Smoked and Fresh (page 85);
Creamy Broccoli Rabe with Pistachios (page 134);
and Savory Cheddar Madeleines (page 198)

needed. I would suggest you do the same with whatever good-quality bread you prefer. This is because good bread, paired with a couple of easy smears or spreads, is the spontaneous snacker's ally. When you want something semisubstantial and not at all boring, pulling more than one flavorful spread out of the fridge is a treat. And while "bread courses" have become trendy in certain circles, I'm partial to choosing one good loaf and saving the variety for what it gets dipped in or smeared with.

The bread and spread affair of which I'm enamored is not to be confused with toasts (which are more composed and have a dedicated chapter all their own coming up). What I'm talking about here is a more casual snacking experience, more akin to a cheese and charcuterie board where you graze from one bite to the next, savoring a different flavor here and a different texture there. The idea is to move beyond the expected sole tub of hummus or single bowl of guacamole in favor of something more diverse, more surprising: A couple or even a few dippable dishes and jars of good things that can be made well in advance and that complement one another is what you're after. You can, of course, buy dips and salsas and smears at the market, but if you have the inclination and a bit of time, making your own is what you want to be doing.

I promise that blitzing up a can of beans with some olive oil and herbs or some frozen peas with Parmesan and butter will be easy, and I swear that tackling a homemade pâté or whipping up a vegetable puree will be healthier for you. Most importantly, any of these will taste infinitely better than anything you can buy at the grocery store. And what's more, it's fun. Set out a bowl of Creamy Broccoli Rabe with Pistachios (page 134) alongside a jar of Harissa-Roasted Tomatoes (page 75), and all you need is a baguette and a butter knife. Offer up a jar of Potted Salmon, Smoked and Fresh (page 85) and a dish of Arugula, White Bean, and Roasted Garlic Smear (page 121), and I guarantee you will surely delight your fellow snackers more than with anything you'll find prepackaged in the deli section.

The Beauty of the Scattered Platter

A bountiful cheese and charcuterie board is sexy for sure, but these days I find those artfully clustered, highly curated boards require almost as much planning, shopping, and arranging as a fully orchestrated menu. Instead, I lean in to the notion of "this is what I have and this is what I want to eat right now." An approach to snacking (and sharing) that I call "the scattered platter."

Unlike the boards and platters that abound online, these are simple gatherings of good things. Often a spread or smear is included, always some fresh fruit or veg (it can be a ripe avocado, some leftover roasted potatoes, or oil-slick sautéed greens, whatever your fridge offers up), definitely something crunchy or salty (think crackers, toasts, breadsticks, even chips), often an egg, usually some cheese, and a few slices of cured meat, some smoked fish, or a slice of pâté.

It may seem random, chaotic, even a little shambolic, but the way I think of it, if it's stuff I like to eat then my friends and family probably will too. It's a perfect way to snack when you're alone but also a get-out-free card for entertaining; there's no need to overthink or color-coordinate it—just pull out a smattering of your favorite things, scatter them on a plate, and call it done. This is not haphazard; on the contrary, it's a nod to intimacy. A scattered platter shared doesn't say you don't care; it says you're comfortable together, that you're a friend as much as a guest.

Embracing Shame-Free Shopping-Only Spreads

If you've peered into my pantry, this will come as no surprise to you: As much as I love to cook and make food, I am also devoted to good-quality products that you can buy and that require little more than the twist of a lid or twirl from the can opener. Some of my go-to snacking spreads are not about cooking, require minimal chopping, and rely almost entirely on clever shopping. And I'm not even slightly embarrassed by this.

The Europeans are way ahead of us when it comes to well-preserved delicacies and have long relied on tinned fish and jarred vegetables to make last-minute snacking both easy and interesting. Look for imported specialties, such as baby clams and mussels, sardines and mackerel, octopus and anchovies—all of which can be served right out of the pretty cans they come in. Try different peppers, pickles, or giardiniera for a bright and crunchy snack that can also be eaten straight from the jar—only toothpicks needed. And while I am not enamored of most packaged crackers, the good, salty, packaged snacks I've found are almost always imports of one kind or another.

It's not that you shouldn't cook (you should!), but if you're a passionate snacker, finding yourself a good imported foods shop (or jumping online) will only add to your repertoire. Mix these specialty goods in with what you've made yourself or serve them totally on their own. I assure you that no one will balk when you set out a dish of Marcona almonds, some good green olives, and a tin of boquerones (fresh anchovies marinated in vinegar) for happy hour. And I guarantee you won't get any complaints if you open a jar of Italian tuna fillets or a can of octopus, add some sun-dried tomatoes in olive oil, a dish of Niçoise olives, and a few slices of toast for a last-minute aperitivo. You don't need this book to help you do this, but it's worth mentioning that snacking does not have to involve a ton of cooking or even prep if you keep your larder stocked with interesting things in jars and tins.

Heirlooms, Odds and Ends, and What Makes It Your Table

Every cook I know has their own personal style, not just what they cook but how they serve it. Some are more formal and fastidious, and others are more laid back and carefree. I know people who wouldn't dream of serving red and white wine out of the same-style glass and others who see no harm in serving gin and tonics out of Solo cups. None of it is right or wrong, just different.

My table tends to go more eclectic than elegant, and I'm comfortable with that. Nothing really matches, and I often don't have the right size plate or bowl for what I'm serving, but I always manage to figure something out. The most important thing, I think, is that your serving ware should match the occasion, not just in terms of style but function too. One large platter makes sense to me when a few good friends come round and it's an intimate, communal thing. When it's just one or two of us, a couple of tiny dishes are perfect for cocktail-hour snacks. And if it's more of a crowd, well, then it might be a napkins-only affair with various bowls and dishes, maybe a bread basket or a serving board to pick from.

As long as what you use to set your table reflects your taste and is adorned with pieces that you love, that's what matters. I often have a couple of basic jam jars set out alongside a plate my mom got at an auction years ago, a cutting board Ken made for us, and a couple of glasses from the thrift shop. Sometimes one or more of our cereal bowls make a showing because they are the best size for spreads and salsas, regardless of the fact that most mornings they're used for our granola and yogurt. And, often as not, the antique dessert forks that my friend Jackie gave us for our wedding are mingled in with a long, serrated baguette knife that cuts cheese as well as a rustic loaf. It's kind of a mess, but it's our mess: things we've collected when we travel, bits we've been given, and all manner of secondhand stuff. Pieces that hold meaning for us, and that, even when they don't match or quite fit the food, definitely communicate that this table really couldn't be anyone else's.

Fig Panzanella with Proscuitto and Goat Cheese (page 162); Favas Fritas with Frizzled Parsley (page 102); and Creamy Broccoli Rabe with Pistachios (page 134)

A Few Notes on the Recipes

I aim to write recipes that give even the most novice cook all the verbal and visual cues needed for the dishes to taste the way they do when I make them. However, unlike restaurant fare where the food is replicated exactly the same way dish after dish, day after day, home cooking is dependent on many variables: the brand of the ingredient used, the calibration of the oven, the hand of the individual cook, and more. With all this in mind, it's inevitable that your food will taste different than mine, and that's perfectly wonderful. In fact, while I do try to provide as much guidance as possible, I also think some aspects of cooking are so personal that they're nearly impossible to quantify, which is why I've included the following notes so you'll know what you'll find in the recipes, and in some cases, what you won't, as you go into this snacking adventure:

- You'll notice I don't give preparation times with my recipes. That's because what takes me five minutes to do might take you twenty—or two. I don't pretend to know how fast you peel garlic or measure flour. What I do suggest, though, is that you read the recipe in its entirety before you begin. There are few things in the kitchen more annoying than starting a recipe and realizing you need two hours for the dough to rise (or in the case of the focaccia recipe here, two days). Most of these recipes are not terribly time intensive, but again, what you and I consider fast (or slow) may well differ.

- For the nonbaking recipes, I offer estimates on how many servings each recipe will provide; however, in most of the baking and dessert recipes I provide actual yields (how many the recipe makes). But keep in mind, how much you eat may vary widely from how much I eat. Most of these recipes are intended for four to eight people to share; if for more, the recipe indicates as such.

- With regard to ingredient amounts, you'll see that when it comes to fresh herbs I suggest "a small handful" or "4 or 5 stems" rather than specific measurements. I also leave salt and pepper and sometimes red pepper flakes and lemon juice "to taste." Again, this is because I think food is very personal, and how much rosemary you like might be considerably different than how much I like. I salt my food quite generously, but you may not. And salts themselves vary in terms of saltiness! Which is why the suggestions for these ingredients are just that: suggestions. I hope you will taste your cooking as you go so that you can decide if you need more or less of any of these flavorings. You'll also see that I offer both grams and cups for baking measurements. Amounts can vary wildly between a cup of flour scooped out of the bag versus an exact weight. If you have a scale, I always recommend weighing ingredients. If you don't, it's not the end of the world, but know that in baking it may well make the difference between a cake being a bit drier or moister or a cracker being a bit more tender or slightly tougher.

- Substitutions are essential to any cook but especially so in the snacker's kitchen because you want to be able to pull stuff together easily, without necessarily having to run to the store for just one ingredient. Nothing in this book is esoteric to my mind, and even I don't keep clotted cream on hand all the time. If you want to make something here and don't have a specific ingredient, I encourage you to substitute something that seems right to you. Ricotta, crème fraîche, and even Greek yogurt can all work as a smear on toast or creamy addition to a spread—they may taste a little sweeter or tangier or buttery-er, but that doesn't mean it won't still be delicious. If you don't have a sweet onion, a yellow or red onion with a dash of sugar will be fine. I often use light and dark brown sugar interchangeably based on what I have. Use what makes the most sense to you, and again, be a little courageous. Sometimes on-the-fly substitutions become go-to solutions.

- Last, I don't include a section on equipment in this book because if you have even the most basic kitchen, you can make 75 percent of what's here. Nothing is too cheffy or rarefied to require investment in a bunch of fancy tools and utensils. If you have basic bowls, pots and pans, and a good knife, you're more than halfway there. However, I do rely on my scale and food processor heavily, adore my mandoline, and think a fine sieve is worth the minimal amount of space it takes up in the drawer. I also use silicone baking sheets and tart rings in a couple of recipes, a pasta maker in one, and piping bags in another. Not having these specific items won't prohibit you from making the recipes if you're really motivated, but they will make it easier. That said, in a pinch, I've used a ziplock bag with the corner cut out for a piping bag, and a rolling pin and a lot of muscle will stand in for a pasta maker.

PAIRING THOUGHTS FOR THE IN-BETWEEN MEAL

There's very little in this collection that won't work together, but to get you started thinking about mixing and mingling different recipes, here are a few of my go-to combos for inspiration.

Meet Me in the Med...

Fig Panzanella with Prosciutto and Goat Cheese (page 162)

Creamy Broccoli Rabe with Pistachios (page 134)

Carta di Musica or other crackers or toasts (page 192)

Melon and coppa

Welcoming Spring on the Patio

Potted Salmon, Smoked and Fresh (page 85)

Jammy Eggs with Fried Shallots (page 113)

Grilled Asparagus and Little Gem Lettuce with Burrata (page 154)

Snap peas and/or radishes with salty butter

Crusty bread

Late-Afternoon Fireside

Duck and Bacon Rillettes with Pistachios (page 80)

Fennel Ratatouille Salsa (page 124)

Grilled toasts

Festive New Year's Day

Tater Tots with Crème Fraîche and Caviar (page 96)

Butter-Poached Lobster on Brioche (page 50)

Chocolate Pots with Boozy Cream (page 224)

Elderflower and Meyer Lemon 75 (page 238)

Lots of Friends, Midsummer

Parmesan Grissini (page 190)

Lots of fresh, crunchy garden vegetables

Antipasto Skewers (page 140)

Watermelon with Marinated Feta and Black Olives (page 149)

Stone Fruit Salad with Tomatoes and Mozzarella (page 161)

Salted Silver-Dollar Ice Cream Sandwiches (page 220)

Celebrating Fall's Arrival

Shaved Brussels Sprouts with Apples and Sheep's Cheese (page 55)

Bacon, Sweet Onion, and Apple Tarts (page 109)

Savory Cheddar Madeleines (page 198)

Fig and Balsamic Jam (page 86)

Last-Minute Glass of Wine on a Wednesday (or Whenever)

Artichoke and Green Olive Tapenade (page 120)

Butter Beans with Asparagus (page 84)

Carta di Musica or other crackers or toasts (page 192)

Snacks By Way of Seville

Favas Fritas with Frizzled Parsley (page 102)

Tortilla with Jamón and Shrimp (page 165)

Spanish-Style BLT (Jamón-Topped Pan con Tomate with Baby Greens) (page 67)

Olives

Aperitivo for Two or More

Tarallini (page 201)

Prosciutto Butter with Asparagus and Arugula (page 64)

Bresaola, Green Olives, and Parmesan (page 142)

Unexpected Pals, Anytime

Gruyère Gougères (page 99)

Champagne

A Picnic Just Because

Fennel-y Garden Pickles (page 82)

Fromager d'Affinois, Apple, and French Ham (page 54)

Double Chocolate Olive Oil Biscotti (page 215)

An Inspired Game-Day Spread

Communal Shrimp and Crab Cocktail via Baja (page 169)

Oaxacan-Style Tlayudas with Mushroom-Quinoa "Chorizo" (page 175)

Creamy Tomatillo Salsa (page 133)

Rhubarb Margarita (page 242)

Movie Night (First Up, *Casablanca*)

Bessara with Harissa (page 127)

Middle Eastern–Style Flatbread (page 195)

Mediterranean Farro Salad with Olives and Parsley (page 167)

Chocolate Zucchini Snacking Cakes (page 214)

Vegetarian Visitors (and Other Picky Eaters)

Forest Floor Pâté (page 77)

Gluten-Free Fennel Crackers (page 203)

Smashed Fava Beans and Peas with Zucchini, Clotted Cream, and Mint (page 61)

Rhubarb-Plum Cobbler Cake (page 231)

With Vegans in Mind

Arugula, White Bean, and Roasted Garlic Smear (page 121)

Harissa-Roasted Tomatoes (page 75)

Focaccia with Caramelized Onions and Thyme (page 185)

Chapter 1

ON TOAST

THERE ARE SOME FOODS YOU SIMPLY NEVER TIRE OF. Foods that make you feel safe when you're wobbly and lure you back to health when you've been ill. Foods that the mere aroma of is enough to help you feel that things off-kilter will right themselves. Onions sautéing in butter in the fall, brazenly strong coffee on a cold morning, bacon anytime—these olfactory experiences all evoke their own comforting responses for me, but it's toast that really does me in.

Whether it's thick slabs of a rustic whole grain, the crust blistered and blackened in spots, or golden slices of a buttery brioche, toast is the simplest of foods, yet it comforts in the most complex way, reaching deep in the crevices of memory to soothe and satiate. And the amazing thing about toast on its own is this: It doesn't have to be great to be really good. What I mean is, sometimes the last heel in a bag, the runt of the loaf left idling in crumbs at the back of the freezer—that sorry piece—once toasted and slathered in salty butter can become all I need at that moment. However, when you're thinking of toast as the vessel for other toppings, as the base of more involved snacks, starting with good stuff does make a difference. For a good toast, you don't want to cover up the flavor of the bread with toppings—what you want is the topping to enhance the toast and vice versa. And by toppings, I mean ingredients that get better when mingled with others, flavors that truly benefit from being blended together or layered on top of one another.

With a good loaf of bread in hand, you can create small miracles simply by giving each slice a quick brush of olive oil or smear of butter, a brief flash under the broiler or on the grill, and then topping it with any number of fresh or cooked vegetables, combinations of cured meats, or myriad melted cheeses. Fish is also a lovely idea, be it tinned or freshly cooked.

In fact, I've found some of my favorite toasts come about when I have a collection of leftovers in need of using up. A few slices of leftover grilled salmon flaked into a bowl, drizzled with lemon juice, and tossed with baby arugula becomes a wonder when mounded on a toothsome baguette. A small dish of roasted romanesco, peppered with leftover sausage and grated Parmesan, spooned on a slice of sourdough is heavenly.

Toasts are a clever way to serve snacks because they come with their own edible plate. Whether you choose to serve large slices, a single piece for each of you, or a bunch of smaller bits to sit side by side with other snacks, the bread gives substance to a snacking event. If I'm having one or two friends around, the toasts I make are likely more of the open-faced sandwich size, but if I'm expecting more of a crowd, slicing a single baguette into many pieces makes more sense. But it's really all up for grabs and that's half the fun of it, because any way you slice it (see what I did there?) there are nearly limitless combinations, and if you use your imagination, along with the following ideas, you'll never tire of toast, in any form.

Butter-Poached Lobster on Brioche

2 lobster tails,
uncooked or cooked

6 tablespoons unsalted
European butter
(such as Kerrygold,
Plugra, Isigny Ste
Mère, or similar)

Sea salt

4 to 6 slices
brioche bread

1 lemon, halved

I'm not going to pretend this doesn't feel a bit fancy (it is lobster, after all), but the preparation is far from fussy: Boil lobster, melt butter, toast bread. You really can't get much simpler and still turn out such an impressive snack (I suppose spooning caviar on crackers might be easier, but only moderately so). And know that you don't have to buy fresh lobster tails and boil them if you don't want to; many grocery stores now sell vacuum-packed preboiled tails. But if you do want to use fresh, don't be intimidated. This isn't boiling a whole, live creature with all the requisite drama that entails; this is just tails— you've got this. Second, if brioche isn't available, don't fret, challah works too. What you want is that rich butter-and-eggs flavor, and while I prefer the lightness of brioche, use what you can find. Don't skimp on the butter, though; good-quality European-style butter makes a big difference, and while it's expensive, if you're splurging on lobster, you might as well treat it well. **MAKES 4 TO 6 TOASTS**

If you're using uncooked lobster tails, bring a large pot of salted water to a boil. Put the lobster tails in the pot and cook them until the shells turn red (a good rule is about 1 minute per ounce of tail, so 5 minutes for a 5-ounce lobster tail is a rough gauge). Remove the tails and let cool before shelling.

When the tails are cool, use kitchen shears to cut the belly side of the tail lengthwise from one end to the other. Carefully, so you don't cut yourself on the shell, open up the lobster as you would a book and tug the meat out—if it's cooked through it will come out quite easily. If it's a bit undercooked, cut the shell along the back side as well to help the meat release (you're going to cook the meat again gently so don't worry if it's a tad underdone).

Cut the lobster into bite-size chunks. In a medium saucepan, melt the butter over medium heat. When the bubbles from the butter have dissipated, lower the heat to medium-low and add the lobster. Sprinkle with salt, then taste and tweak the seasoning if needed.

Preheat the broiler. Lightly toast the brioche, keeping an eye on it as the high butter content will help it brown quickly.

When the lobster is warmed through, spoon a few pieces onto each toast and drizzle with some of the butter. Squeeze a bit of lemon over each toast and serve.

Sesame-Spiced Crab Salad

6 ounces fresh or canned lump crabmeat, picked over for shells and cartilage

1 Thai chile, or a small piece of a jalapeño if not available, finely chopped

1 green onion, white and light green parts, finely chopped

Small handful of fresh cilantro, leaves and stems finely chopped

1 tablespoon toasted sesame oil, plus more as needed

Sea salt and freshly ground black pepper

4 to 6 slices rustic bread

Extra-virgin olive oil

Toasted sesame seeds for garnish

My feeling about crab is that it's always quite expensive yet inconsistently delicious. Sadly, I think this is the way of the world now when it comes to much of our food, and shellfish specifically seem to really be suffering (don't get me started on finding flavorful shrimp these days). Whether I buy fresh crab from my fishmonger or opt for the (still not cheap) canned crab at the market, it always seems to be a roll of the dice as to whether it will have any deep crab flavor. Which is unfortunate because when crab is good and sweet, it needs almost nothing added to it but maybe a sprinkle of salt and good squeeze of lemon or lime. That said, I do find that a drizzle of toasted sesame oil, a little heat from a chile, and the freshness of some cilantro will make good crab fabulous and just-okay crab very good (the sesame oil, used sparingly, is the key here). Spooned on toast and sprinkled with sesame seeds, this is a super simple way to bring out the best in crab or save it from mediocrity.

MAKES 4 TO 6 TOASTS

Gently pat the crab dry between paper towels to drain any excess liquid. In a medium bowl, combine the crab, chile, green onion, cilantro, and sesame oil and season with salt and pepper. Taste and add more sesame oil or seasoning as desired.

Brush each slice of bread with the olive oil and then toast until golden brown. Spoon the salad onto the toasted bread, sprinkle with the sesame seeds, and serve.

Sardine Rillettes
with Avocado and Fennel

Two 3.75-ounce cans
sardines in olive oil

½ medium shallot,
finely chopped

1 tablespoon unsalted
butter, softened

Zest and juice of
½ lemon

Sea salt and freshly
ground black pepper

1 small fennel bulb,
trimmed, halved and
cored, fronds reserved

1 avocado, halved,
pitted, and diced small

8 to 12 slices baguette
or 4 to 6 slices rustic
bread, toasted

Sardines, like anchovies, tend to be dismissed out of hand by the uninitiated as too fishy, too oily, too *something*. But here's the thing: Not only are they delicious (give them a chance), they are also an unsung hero of the snacker's pantry. All that bold, briny, complex flavor, all that delicate, meaty texture, is captured in a convenient (and often very beautiful) tin that sits in your cupboard awaiting the moment when you realize you need something exactly that savory and substantial to put on toast. And while traditional rillettes are a way to preserve meat in fat, here I use just a little bit of butter to smooth out the flake of the fish so it spreads nicely and a good dose of lemon to round out the more oceanic edges. If you grew up eating sardines on Triscuits with a squeeze of lemon like I did (and if you didn't, bear with me here), then you'll recognize those rustic snacks as the harbinger of these toasts. The citrus is still there, but tissue-thin slices of fennel and creamy avocado mounded on top of the sardines become a salad of sorts, turning an admittedly retro snack into something familiar but slightly more sophisticated. Don't misunderstand me: I love the simplicity of a just-out-of-the-can, slick-with-oil sardine, an aggressive squeeze of lemon forcing you to eat quickly before the cracker wilts under the weight of it all. To my mind, that's the blue jeans and T-shirt of sardine snacks; think of this as the little black dress. **MAKES 4 TO 6 TOASTS**

Drain the sardines and put them in a medium bowl along with about 2 tablespoons of the oil they're packed with. Use a fork to roughly mash the sardines, then add the softened butter and lemon zest and continue to mash until you have a relatively uniform but still chunky consistency; if they seem dry, add a teaspoon or more of the oil to lightly moisten. Finely chop a small handful of the reserved fennel fronds and mix in gently. Set aside.

Use a mandoline to cut the fennel halves into paper-thin slices, then transfer to a medium bowl. Add the diced avocado and lemon juice and season with salt and pepper. Toss gently to combine.

To serve, spread the sardine mixture on the toasts, top each with a mound of the fennel-avocado mixture, and garnish with more fennel fronds.

Fromager d'Affinois, Apple, and French Ham

½ pound Fromager d'Affinois

6 to 8 slices rustic bread, toasted

1 crisp apple (such as Pippin, Honeycrisp, or similar), thinly sliced

¼ pound French ham, very thinly sliced

This probably shouldn't be called a recipe because you don't need accurate proportions to make it wonderful. You just need the four key ingredients, and you can honestly put them together in almost any form and it'll be perfect. However, spreading the cheese on the bread first offers the apples something to cling to, and when layered in this order, your taste buds are rewarded with a really beautiful succession of flavors: first the smoky ham, then the tart apple, quickly followed by the sweet-earthy cheese. That said, if you simply put these four ingredients out on a picnic blanket and skip the pomp and circumstance I suggest here, you'll still be happy. **MAKES 6 TO 8 TOASTS**

Cut the cheese into ¼-inch slices and gently smear on the toasted bread (don't be afraid to include the soft, outer rind here, as it's completely edible and delicious). Layer the toasts with a few slices of the apple and then top by draping a slice or two of the ham over the apple. Serve with any leftover cheese and apple slices on the side for snacking.

Shaved Brussels Sprouts with Apples and Sheep's Cheese

1 pound brussels sprouts

1 crisp apple (such as Honeycrisp, Granny Smith, or similar)

4 ounces Ossau-Iraty or other medium-firm sheep's milk cheese

½ cup olive oil

Zest and juice of 2 lemons (about ¼ cup juice)

1 tablespoon red wine vinegar, plus more as needed

Pinch of flaky sea salt and freshly ground black pepper

8 to 12 slices baguette or 4 to 6 slices rustic bread, toasted

Brussels sprouts can be polarizing; people seem to either love them or really find them off-putting. I happen to love them in almost any form, and while the more common approach is to cook them, they do very well raw when treated properly. Thinly shaved on a mandoline, the sturdy sprouts take on a feathery lightness that needs only some bright dressing to soften their more cruciferous edges. And while you don't need to make it way ahead of time, you do want to give the sprouts at least a half hour or so to soften in the dressing. The cheese is important too: I've substituted Parmesan in a pinch, but a medium-firm cheese offers the creaminess that you want to balance out the crunch of the sprouts and apples. MAKES 4 TO 6 TOASTS

Using a mandoline, shave the brussels sprouts as finely as you can—you want them to be nearly paper thin. (Alternatively, you can do this with a very sharp knife, but it's much easier and faster with a mandoline and a safety glove.) Transfer the sprouts to a large bowl.

To julienne the apple, first cut the sides off the apple in four sections, leaving just the core behind. Run these four bits through the mandoline on a slightly thicker setting than used for the sprouts; you should end up with very thin half-moons. Stack a few half-moons on top of one another and use a knife to cut those stacks into matchsticks. Toss these in the bowl with the sprouts.

You want the cheese to be very thin as well so it blends in and becomes sort of creamy in contrast to the vegetables. Use a vegetable peeler to take wide but thin sheets off the wedge and then just tear them up into smaller pieces. Set the cheese aside while you make the dressing.

To make the dressing, combine the olive oil, lemon zest and juice, and vinegar in a lidded jar (8 to 12 ounces) and shake to combine. Taste for acidity and add more vinegar, if desired. Drizzle about two-thirds of the dressing over the sprout mixture, season with salt and pepper, and toss to combine. Let sit for at least 30 minutes to macerate. After the sprouts have had a chance to soften in the dressing, taste again and, if needed, add more dressing. Add the reserved cheese, toss, season with salt and pepper, and spoon onto the toasted bread slices to serve.

Wilted Chard
with Mushrooms and Gruyère

¼ cup extra-virgin olive oil, plus more as needed

1 medium shallot, very thinly sliced

Sea salt and freshly ground black pepper

8 to 10 mushrooms (any combination of trumpet, cremini, shiitake, or other), stemmed and quartered

3 to 4 sprigs fresh thyme, leaves picked

½ bunch of green or rainbow chard, stemmed and cut into 1-inch ribbons

1 teaspoon sherry vinegar

2 to 4 thick slices rustic bread, toasted

About ½ cup grated Gruyère cheese

There's always one day, usually mid- to late September, when the air changes; it's no longer swollen with summer's humidity, but full of the snap and crackle of fall. This change in light and the briskness of the breeze is always tinged with a hint of melancholy. But fall, even with its more somber mood (it is after all, the bearer of the news that winter is forthcoming), offers its own delights. As September's perfect tomatoes fade, autumn brings the promise of sturdy greens and earthy mushrooms, flavors designed to distract us from the loss of long, sunny days. This toast is the antidote to the end-of-summer blues; a mash-up of toasted bread, caramelized mushrooms, pungent chard wilted in oil, and nutty Gruyère (or any melty cheese you like). Taken together this simple snack is enough to make summer's departure slightly less heartbreaking. MAKES 2 TO 4 TOASTS

In a large saucepan, heat 2 tablespoons olive oil over medium-high heat. When the oil is hot, add the shallot and sprinkle with salt and pepper. Reduce the heat to medium and cook, stirring frequently, until the shallot begins to color, about 5 minutes. If the pan is dry, add an extra tablespoon of oil.

When the shallot is golden brown on the edges or even beginning to stick to the pan, add the mushrooms and thyme and cook, stirring frequently, until the mushrooms release their juices and start to caramelize, 10 to 12 minutes. Transfer the vegetables to a plate and set aside.

In the same pan, heat the remaining 2 tablespoons olive oil over medium heat. When it shimmers, add the chard in batches until the leaves begin to wilt so they all fit in the pan and cook, stirring occasionally, until they release their liquid, about 5 minutes. Take the pan off the heat and, using a wooden spoon or silicone spatula, gently press the chard against the side of the pan to drain off any excess liquid.

Return the shallot mixture to the pan and stir to combine. Add the vinegar, taste, and season again with salt and pepper.

Preheat the broiler. Arrange the toasts on a baking sheet and top with the vegetable mixture and grated cheese. Place the toasts under the broiler to melt the cheese. Serve immediately.

Smashed Fava Beans and Peas with Zucchini, Clotted Cream, and Mint

1 small zucchini, halved lengthwise and thinly sliced

Zest and juice of 1 lemon

¼ cup extra-virgin olive oil

Pinch of red pepper flakes

Sea salt and freshly ground black pepper

2 pounds fava beans, in their pods

1 pound fresh peas, in their pods

Small handful of mint leaves, or to taste, finely chopped, plus more for garnish

8 to 12 slices baguette or 4 to 6 slices rustic bread, toasted

½ to 1 cup clotted cream

Clotted cream is an English thing. I first had it sitting riverside with a scone and jam a lifetime ago when I briefly lived in London. What struck me about it then, and what still does, is how ridiculously decadent it is. It's not a workaday ingredient like butter. It doesn't have the distinct flavor of a spreadable cheese like ricotta or mascarpone, and unlike yogurt, there's no conceivable way to rationalize it as even the least bit healthy. Maybe crème fraîche comes closest in terms of blatant lusciousness. But regardless, clotted cream is impossible to resist and never more so than when paired with anything green and lemony to counter its rich, fatty flavor. When summer vegetables hit their peak and it's way too hot to turn on the oven, this is a toast you'll want to make. Yes, the favas and the peas demand a little work on the front end (you have to shell both and then, in the case of the favas, blanch the inner beans and peel off the outer skin), but this is the kind of kitchen work that I like, the kind that makes me feel connected to the food. That may sound affected, but with so much of our produce prepeeled, precut, and wrapped up in plastic these days, actually shelling peas and peeling beans slows me down and forces me to engage, even for just a few seconds, with each pod. Side note: I once read that Alice Waters loves to wash lettuce. I don't know if that's strictly true, but I know that I do not. When I wash lettuce, I remind myself that Alice Waters loves it, so I too should make an effort to enjoy it. To me, washing lettuce is a necessity but it doesn't soothe my soul the way shelling peas does. Point being this: If your bliss is not in shelling peas, you can, of course, buy them packaged. **MAKES 4 TO 8 TOASTS**

In a small bowl, combine the zucchini with half the lemon juice, half the olive oil, and the red pepper flakes. Season with salt and black pepper and let sit so the flavors blend.

Meanwhile, bring a medium pot of salted water to a boil and shell the beans and peas. Blanch the fava beans until they float and

(recipe continues)

the outer skin is easily pierced with a knife, about 2 minutes. Use a slotted spoon to transfer the beans to a colander and run under water until they are cool enough to handle. Peel away the second skin of the favas and transfer the beans to a medium bowl. Using the same pot of water, blanch the peas for 2 minutes, then drain and add to the bowl with the beans.

Use a potato masher or fork to lightly mash the beans, peas, and mint with a sprinkle of salt. Mix in some black pepper, the lemon zest, and the remaining lemon juice and olive oil. Add the bean and pea mixture to the zucchini and stir to combine well. Taste and adjust the seasoning as needed.

To serve, spread some clotted cream on each piece of bread, top with a generous scoop of the vegetable mixture, and garnish with additional mint.

Garlicky Rabe
with Sweet Soppressata

1 bunch of broccoli
rabe, trimmed

¼ cup extra-virgin
olive oil, plus more
for drizzling

3 garlic cloves

Sea salt

1 tablespoon fennel
seeds, roughly ground
in a mortar with a pestle
or chopped

¼ to ½ teaspoon
red pepper flakes,
or to taste

1 stick sweet
soppressata (about
6 ounces), peeled and
cut into ¼-inch chunks

4 to 6 slices rustic
bread, toasted

1 cup ricotta cheese

Freshly shaved
Parmesan for garnish

The simplicity and purity of greens, especially heartier ones like rabe that aren't fleeting when cooked and can stand up to other bold flavors, is something I crave. And when layered on a slab of crusty toast with creamy ricotta and a tumble of soppressata, this combination checks every box. One tip: Because we eat a lot of broccoli rabe, I buy two bunches at a time and blanch them till crisp-tender together in a big pot. After draining and squeezing them of excess water, I portion out the rabe and freeze smaller bunches so I can readily add them to pizzas and pastas, blitz them up into Creamy Broccoli Rabe with Pistachios (page 134), and, of course, make this toast. **MAKES 4 TO 6 TOASTS**

Bring a large pot of salted water to a boil. Add the broccoli rabe, stir, and cook until the water returns to a boil and the rabe is bright green with barely tender stems, 3 to 4 minutes. Drain and run under cold water to slow the cooking process. Let cool, then squeeze to remove any excess liquid. Roughly chop the rabe, keeping some of the leaves and florets intact.

In a large skillet or sauté pan, heat the oil over medium heat. Grate the garlic into the skillet and sauté, stirring frequently, until just fragrant, about a minute, turning down the heat as needed to prevent browning. Add the fennel seeds and red pepper flakes and continue cooking for another minute or so before adding the rabe. Toss the rabe in the oil and spice mixture, season with salt, and continue to cook over medium-low heat, stirring frequently, until the rabe is warmed through.

Add the soppressata to the pan, tossing well to combine. Once the soppressata is glossy from the oil and the mixture is warm, 3 to 5 minutes, taste and adjust the seasoning.

Spread the ricotta on the toasts, scoop a generous portion of the rabe mixture on top of each, and drizzle with a bit more olive oil. Finish with the freshly shaved Parmesan and serve.

Prosciutto Butter with Asparagus and Arugula

4 ounces sliced prosciutto

1 tablespoon unsalted European butter (such as Kerrygold, Plugra, Isigny Ste Mère, or similar)

Sea salt

6 to 8 slices rustic bread, toasted

4 to 6 spears asparagus, blanched and cut into 2-inch pieces

1 or 2 handfuls of arugula leaves

Extra-virgin olive oil for drizzling

Juice of ½ lemon for drizzling

I love butter. So much in fact that I'm regularly scolded by Ken for eating it all by itself. I'd say it's a guilty pleasure except that I never feel guilty about it; some people dip a spoon into a pint of ice cream when they walk by the freezer, while others palm a handful of potato chips, and I skim a bit of butter. I also love charcuterie and have a distinct soft spot for prosciutto. Like butter, I am prone to swiping a slice of the sweet, salty, fat-streaked meat nestled between layers of white butcher paper without penance. This recipe is the love child of those two delights, and when slathered (yes, rather thickly) on good sourdough bread and topped with asparagus and arugula, it's joyful. If you're familiar with 'nduja, then this will seem a logical (and good) idea to you. And if you've never made a compound butter before, this may lead you down the path to further decadence; herbs, aromatics, vegetables, nuts, cheeses—you can add myriad ingredients to butter to make it even more delicious. Or just grab a small spoonful all on its own. **MAKES 6 TO 8 TOASTS**

Stack the slices of prosciutto on top of one another, wrap them in plastic wrap, and transfer them to the freezer for about 1 hour (you want the prosciutto firm but not rock-solid). When the prosciutto is quite firm, remove it from the freezer and roughly chop it. Transfer the chopped meat to the bowl of a food processor, add the butter, and pulse the butter and prosciutto together until well combined; it should be spreadable and almost pink uniformly. Add a sprinkle of salt, taste, and adjust the seasoning.

When ready to serve, let the prosciutto butter soften a bit, then spread a generous amount on each slice of toast. Top the prosciutto butter with a couple pieces of asparagus and a few leaves of arugula. Add a very gentle drizzle of olive oil and a squeeze of lemon to serve. Store leftover prosciutto butter in an airtight container in the fridge for up to 1 week.

*Also pictured:
Butter Beans
with Asparagus
(page 84)*

Spanish-Style BLT
(Jamón-Topped Pan con Tomate with Baby Greens)

2 large ripe tomatoes

3 to 4 good-quality anchovy fillets

Sea salt and freshly ground black pepper

4 to 6 slices rustic bread

Extra-virgin olive oil, as needed

2 or so large garlic cloves

4 to 6 thin slices jamón

A few good handfuls of arugula or other baby lettuce

Green olives (such as Cerignola, Castelvetrano, or other) for serving

Like most cooks, I tend to feel the need to tweak things, sometimes just a little (a bit more cheese, a little longer in the oven) and sometimes a lot (twice as many mushrooms, half as much cream). Making a recipe your own is part of the cooking process, the creative part, and it's how we invent our own personal food lexicon, how we find the recipes that become our keepers. This is an open-faced sandwich that started as one thing and has evolved over time into something quite different. It began as a pan con tomate (the classic Catalan toast) before it was layered with jamón (Spanish dried cured ham) and topped with delicate baby greens and doused with olive oil. Like the classic preparation, the tomato is grated into a pulp and the anchovies are lightly smashed. The garlic is fresh if you like a bit of fire or you can roast it for an earthier flavor. The jamón is chiffon-thin, so it lies in gentle ruffles on top of the tomato-laden toast, and the greens are whatever you choose (I like arugula for a bit of spice). Served with meaty green olives in lieu of pickles, it's not a traditional BLT—or a conventional pan con tomate—but it is a keeper.

MAKES 4 TO 6 TOASTS

Set a box grater inside a large bowl and grate the tomatoes using the side with the largest holes. Grate as much of each tomato as possible, until all that's left is the remnant of some skin (which you can discard); you should have a pulpy, juicy mixture.

Add the anchovies to the grated tomato and mash them up until they're relatively well blended with the tomato pulp. Taste and add a pinch or more of salt if necessary and a generous grind of pepper.

To serve, brush the bread with olive oil on one side and toast. Then halve the garlic and rub the cut side of a clove over the top of each piece of toast to impart flavor; discard the garlic. Smear each toast with a layer of the tomato mixture. Drape a piece of the jamón on the bread, mound with the arugula, and finish with a drizzle of the olive oil. Serve with olives on the side.

Brioche Banh Mi
with Spicy Mayo

Pickles

½ cup distilled
white vinegar

½ cup unseasoned
rice vinegar

1 cup water

¼ cup sugar

1½ tablespoons sea salt

1 bay leaf,
preferably fresh

1 dried red chile

1 medium daikon radish,
peeled and julienned

2 to 3 medium carrots,
peeled and julienned

Spicy Mayo

½ cup mayonnaise

1 tablespoon sambal
oelek (or other chili
paste)

2 green onions,
finely diced

Toasts

4 to 6 slices brioche

8 ounces liverwurst

2 Persian cucumbers,
sliced into rounds

2 jalapeños, thinly
sliced (optional)

3 or 4 stems cilantro,
leaves picked

I should probably be embarrassed to admit this, but I was that kid who loved liverwurst. In elementary school, my favorite sandwich was sliced egg bread smeared with French's yellow mustard and a round of liverwurst, the little white ring of plasticky paper that surrounded each slice removed, and the patty pressed firmly into the soft bread (two slices if no one was looking). I'm inclined to say that this demonstrates what a sophisticated palate I had at eight years old, my affinity for what is essentially pâté shining through even as a third grader. But I think that's probably revisionist history—I just liked liverwurst and still do. This abridged version of a banh mi, featuring deli counter liverwurst standing in for fancier pâté, indulges my childlike tendencies. The brioche is also clearly not traditional (for a real banh mi, the bread should of course be Vietnamese baguette), but it harkens back to the seeded egg bread I used to carry to school and offers a little bit of fatty sweetness to balance out the spicy mayo and tangy pickle—both of which are very quick and easy to make yourself. MAKES 4 TO 6 TOASTS

In a small saucepan, combine the vinegars and water. Set the pan over high heat, add the sugar, salt, bay leaf, and chile, and bring to a boil. Stir to dissolve the sugar, then lower the heat to medium. Add the radish and carrots and cook until the radish is slightly translucent and the carrots have softened but aren't mushy, 1 to 2 minutes. Remove from the heat and let cool.

In a small bowl, stir together the mayo, sambal oelek, and green onions until well combined.

Preheat the broiler. Lightly toast the brioche, keeping an eye on it as the high butter content will help it brown quickly.

Spread the prepared mayo on the toasted brioche and top each with some of the liverwurst, a slice or two of cucumber, a generous scoop of the radish and carrot pickles, jalapeños (if using), and a few cilantro leaves. Store any leftover pickles in an airtight container in the fridge for up to 1 week.

Chapter 2

IN JARS

SOME PEOPLE SHOW UP WITH WINE; OTHERS BRING FLOWERS. I have been known to arrive at the door bearing Mason jars filled with rillettes or red onion jam. You don't always know how it will land, offering your host a jar of something rather than a bottle or a bouquet, but generally I find people are pleasantly surprised. So much so in fact that, once, a friend who was getting married and having a rather casual outdoor soiree in Vermont asked me to bring large jars of preserved lemons and the aforementioned savory jam in lieu of a gift, a request so touching that I took it as license to continue showing up at hosts' homes with these less-than-conventional treats in hand.

So if you invite me over, be warned, you may receive a pot of pâté or a jar of jam or some marinated vegetable as my way of saying thank you. That's because there's something both surprising and old-timey about a jar that I love. Like a quilt or a handknit sweater (with a lot less work), a jar of something feels personal—it says you put a bit of time and energy into it, went a little beyond just hitting the shops on your way over.

But beyond being a nice gift, jars are a highly practical addition to the snacker's repertoire. The same delicacies that I make to give away are the ones I want to eat myself. And whether it's a quick pickle or a creamy pâté, a savory spread or a sweet jam, the kinds of foods that are best suited to jars are the kind that you make ahead of time to have at the ready—whether that's to accompany a full spread for many or as something to dip into on the fly when you're solo.

The other nifty thing about jars is that there's no plating needed. They look great on a table—whether what you have is a simple Mason jar or a special vintage find—you don't have to think about "how to serve" it when it's already in a jar. Just set them out and fill in the gaps with whatever makes sense in terms of accompaniment. The jars I use range in size from 4 to 32 ounces and include everything from classic canning jars to the more refined German-made Weck

versions, as well as those ubiquitous gingham-lidded jam jars that seem to reproduce in the cupboard and are brilliant for making salad dressing. But since the last thing I want you to do is go buy jars, use whatever sizes you have and mix and mingle them freely. Whether you choose to put out a few different jars of this and that or just one with a side of some bread or crackers, snacking from jars is often unexpected but always inviting.

One thing worth noting is that some of the recipes here are slightly more involved than in other chapters— pâtés do take a little work, some marinated vegetables benefit from being roasted or braised first, and even the pickles and jams need a few minutes on the stove. But don't let this deter you. The end results you'll get from a modicum of time and effort will make these snacks look and, most importantly, taste extra special.

Also pictured: Marinated Baby Artichokes (page 76); Potted Salmon, Smoked and Fresh (page 85); and Butter Beans with Asparagus (page 84)

Harissa-Roasted Tomatoes

8 plum tomatoes, quartered

2 garlic cloves, smashed

2 tablespoons extra-virgin olive oil

1 tablespoon balsamic vinegar, plus more as needed

2 tablespoons harissa

½ teaspoon sugar, plus more as needed

⅛ teaspoon red pepper flakes, or to taste

Sea salt and freshly ground black pepper

Most cooks I know have a few pantry ingredients that they lean on regularly to give things a bit of added oomph. One of my oomph-ingredients is harissa, a North African chile paste that you can buy by the jar. I find harissa adds a warming, aromatic, not overly spicy layer to all sorts of things. You'll see later on that I (rather unconventionally) use it in my Bessara with Harissa (page 127), I frequently spoon some into my burgers, and regularly slather it on carrots before roasting them. But harissa really works wonders when paired with roasted tomatoes, as the juice from the fruit mingles happily with the chile paste to create a savory jam. Serve this as a chunky dip for bread or as a relish, like you would caponata.

SERVES 4 TO 6

Preheat the oven to 375°F. Put the tomato pieces and garlic on a large baking sheet and drizzle with the olive oil and vinegar. Spoon the harissa on the tomatoes and sprinkle with the sugar and red pepper flakes. Use your hands to gently toss the tomatoes in the dressing until well coated, then sprinkle lightly with salt and black pepper.

Transfer the baking sheet to the oven and roast until the tomatoes are beginning to caramelize on the edges and the juices have been released and start to thicken, about 30 minutes. When the tomatoes begin to stick to the pan a bit and the juices are slightly jammy, remove the tray from the oven. Taste and adjust the seasoning if needed, adding more sugar or more vinegar, salt or black pepper. Transfer the mixture to a lidded jar (24 to 32 ounces) and serve either at room temperature or chilled. Once cooled, store in an airtight container in the fridge for up to 1 week.

Marinated Baby Artichokes

12 baby artichokes

2 garlic cloves, smashed

½ to ¾ cup extra-virgin olive oil

Juice of 1 lemon

1 teaspoon sea salt, or more to taste

For years I used to buy marinated artichokes from my local Italian specialty store in New York City. These were nothing like the kind you get in a jar at the grocery store. They were the long-stemmed kind, submerged in a tangy marinade, the kind you see in Italy or Spain, elegantly long thistles bobbing in a slick of oil and herbs, which the guys behind the counter would fish out for me one by one and sell by the quart. They were an extravagance for sure, but they made everything, from pasta to pizza to salads to a snack straight out of the plastic tub, pure heaven. In fact, as we cut them up, Ken and I had a ritual of sharing the long-stemmed portion as a pre-dinner perk, the perfect stove-side bite. Then, during the pandemic, when our shopping routines were stymied, I missed these delicacies so much I decided to try to emulate them at home. I started simply, with a few of the key flavors and then adjusted until it seemed the balance of oil to lemon, garlic to salt, was just right. Also, I'm owning up now to laziness when it comes to acidulated water. I don't bother with it. Yes, the artichokes color a bit while you're trimming them, and I agree, it's not a pretty shade of blue-gray. But you're going to boil them and marinate them, and they won't hold their green anyway, so I save the step (and the lemon), and in the end nobody really seems to mind.

SERVES 6 TO 8

Bring a large pot of salted water to a boil. Meanwhile, remove the outer leaves of the artichokes until you reach the inner, more tender center. Trim the bottoms and tops. Add the artichokes to the boiling water and cook until they can be easily pierced with a paring knife, 6 to 8 minutes, depending on how small your artichokes are.

Drain the artichokes. When they're cool enough to handle, halve them and transfer them to a medium bowl or glass storage container. Add the garlic, olive oil, lemon juice, and salt. Taste—you want a sprightly marinade so it penetrates the artichokes. Make sure all the artichokes are fully covered in the marinade. Cover the bowl and refrigerate overnight. Transfer the artichokes and their marinade to a lidded jar (16 to 24 ounces) and return to the fridge until ready to serve; they will keep for up to 1 week in the fridge.

Forest Floor Pâté

2 tablespoons
extra-virgin olive oil,
plus more as needed

3 tablespoons unsalted
butter

3 garlic cloves, smashed

1 medium shallot,
chopped

1 pound fresh
mushrooms (such
as cremini, shiitake,
oyster, chanterelle,
or a combination),
quartered

Sea salt and freshly
ground black pepper

5 to 6 sprigs thyme

Splash of white wine
or cognac

½ cup walnuts,
lightly toasted

Mushrooms have been around for about eight hundred million years (truly), before plants and long before we were on the scene. Yet recently they seem to be having a moment; books and documentaries abound about these magical, mystical forest dwellers, and foraging for fungi is de rigueur among those smart enough (or brave enough) to know their Morchella from their Amanita. I admit I'm enchanted by mushrooms, not just their myriad earthy flavors and meaty textures but their quirky woodland beauty as well. Some people love guests to show up with a bottle or a bouquet, but bring me a handful of hen of the woods or a cluster of chestnut mushrooms any day and I'm slayed. Shiitake, trumpet, oyster, and even the quotidian cremini make me happy. This fungi-forward pâté gives me free rein to use whatever is available, but I lean toward the more affordable here, as the other ingredients add enough flavor that you don't need to buy the fanciest and you'll still get a rich, savory spread. SERVES 4 TO 6

Preheat the oven to 400°F.

In a large oven-safe lidded saucepan or Dutch oven, heat the olive oil and 2 tablespoons of the butter over medium-high heat. Add the garlic and shallot and sauté until just fragrant, about 2 minutes. Add the mushrooms and cook until they just begin to soften, about 3 minutes, adding a bit more oil if they seem dry. Sprinkle with salt and pepper. Add the thyme sprigs, cover the pan, and transfer it to the oven to roast until the mushrooms are cooked through and the garlic is very soft and fragrant, about 20 minutes. Remove from the oven and discard the thyme stems.

Set the pan over medium-high heat and add the wine to deglaze; cook until the liquid has nearly evaporated. Transfer the mushroom mixture to the bowl of a food processor, add the walnuts, and blitz until the mixture is almost smooth, 30 seconds to 1 minute. Add the remaining 1 tablespoon butter and continue to process until the mixture is fully combined and very smooth.

Use a silicone spatula to transfer the puree to a lidded jar (12 to 14 ounces) and tamp down the puree as best you can. Seal the jar and let it set up in the fridge for a few hours or, better, overnight. To serve, bring the pâté to room temperature. Store pâté in an airtight container in the fridge for up to 1 week.

Duck and Bacon Rillettes with Pistachios

2 slices thick-cut bacon, preferably frozen

2 duck legs confit

¼ cup unsalted butter, plus 1 tablespoon, softened

2 tablespoons dry white wine

3 to 4 sprigs thyme, leaves picked

½ teaspoon Dijon mustard

½ teaspoon whole-grain mustard

¼ cup pistachios, toasted and chopped

Sea salt and freshly ground black pepper

One character trait I find common among my friends who love to cook is that they also love to tinker. Never fully satisfied to just take a recipe at face value, many of us feel that pull to try to make it just a little better or just a bit different. I am notorious for fooling around with a recipe just for the sake of it when inspiration hits. Sometimes this leads to deep disappointment where I silently (and sometimes not so silently) berate myself. *Why did you have to mess with it when it was just fine as it was?* I admonish, wishing I could just undo what I've done instead of starting all over again. But then there are the other times (like this one) when a recipe I think is totally solid might still get even better—and it does. Here I've taken my standby clementine and cognac-spiked duck rillettes and gussied them up with bacon and pistachios instead. They are still very simple—I use store-bought duck confit so the only real cooking is the bacon—but the addition of that bit of pork flavor and the nutty pistachios gives them a welcome complexity. And yes, I use two different kinds of mustard; the Dijon adds to the creaminess and the whole grain offers a snappy brightness. However, if you have only one of the two, just double up on that one and it'll still be lovely. **SERVES 6 TO 8**

Julienne the bacon as thinly as possible, about 1/16 inch thick (it's much easier to do this if your bacon is frozen). Then cut the julienne crosswise into pieces about the size of grains of rice. Put the bacon in a small sauté pan set over medium-low heat and cook, rendering the fat slowly, until the meat is browned but not crisp, about 6 minutes. Transfer the bacon and the rendered fat to the bowl of a stand mixer fitted with the paddle attachment; reserve the pan.

Remove the meat from the duck legs, separating any excess fat, discarding the bones and fat, and tearing the meat into large pieces. Add the duck and ¼ cup of the butter to the mixer with the bacon. Run the mixer on low speed for a minute to break up the duck meat and begin to combine it with the butter and bacon. Increase the speed to medium and continue to mix until the duck meat begins to shred, about 2 minutes.

Pour the wine into the pan you used to cook the bacon and place it over medium-high heat. Cook until the wine begins to reduce a bit and the alcohol has burned off, about 30 seconds. Add the wine to the mixer along with the thyme and both mustards (if you don't have both kinds of mustard, don't worry, just use a full teaspoon of whichever you have).

Continue to mix until the meat is finely shredded and fully combined with the butter and other ingredients; it should be spreadable. Add the pistachios and season with salt and pepper, taste, and adjust the seasoning as needed.

Transfer the rillettes to a lidded jar (12 to 14 ounces), pack tightly, and smooth the top. In a small saucepan, melt the remaining tablespoon of butter over low heat and pour the fat over the top of the rillettes to create a seal. Cover the jar and keep refrigerated, making sure to bring it to room temperature before serving. Store leftover rillettes in an airtight container in the fridge for up to 1 week.

Fennel-y Garden Pickles

½ medium fennel bulb, trimmed and cored, fronds reserved

½ English cucumber, or 2 Persian cucumbers

1 small red onion

3 or 4 small radishes, halved

1 cup distilled white vinegar

1 cup water

¼ cup sugar

1½ tablespoons sea salt

1 bay leaf, preferably fresh

1 teaspoon fennel seeds

1 dried red chile (optional)

There are two things about this pickle recipe that make me very happy: First, as the name indicates, it's a fennel-forward concoction. Not only is fresh fennel what you're pickling, but you're also adding fennel seeds to the brine to boost that lovely licorice back note, and fennel fronds are added at the end to further punctuate it. Second, it's pretty; the red onion and radish both exude just enough of their natural color to turn the liquid—and the vegetables—a nice, soft shade of pink. All this plus, by slicing the vegetables very thinly, everything maintains a welcome delicacy, so it's subtle enough to serve on top of a toast or as part of a scattered platter. **SERVES 6 TO 8**

Cut the fennel into quarters, then use a mandoline to slice the quarters into very thin pieces. Using a knife or adjusting the mandoline, cut the cucumber into ¼-inch-thin disks and slice the onion into ⅛-inch-thin half-moons.

In a medium saucepan, combine the vinegar, water, sugar, salt, bay leaf, fennel seeds, and chile (if using) and bring to a boil. Stir the mixture to dissolve the sugar and salt, then add the vegetables. Lower the heat to medium and simmer the vegetables until they have softened slightly, about 1 minute. Remove the pan from the heat and let the vegetables steep until they come to room temperature.

Add the reserved fennel fronds to the cooled mixture, then transfer everything to a lidded jar (24 to 32 ounces) and put the pickles in the fridge to chill. Store the pickles in an airtight container in the fridge for up to 1 week.

Butter Beans with Asparagus

6 to 8 slender asparagus spears, trimmed and halved

One 14-ounce can butter beans or cannellini beans, rinsed and drained, or equivalent dry beans after cooking

½ to ¾ cup extra-virgin olive oil

1 small shallot, finely minced

Zest and juice of 1 lemon

3 garlic cloves, smashed

6 to 8 pepperoncini, trimmed and finely chopped

1 to 2 tablespoons roughly chopped fresh oregano

½ teaspoon red pepper flakes, or to taste

1 teaspoon red wine vinegar or brining liquid from the pepperoncini

Sea salt and freshly ground black pepper

I've been making various versions of these beans for years now and they never cease to make people happy. There's something about the way the marinade infuses itself into the beans that just makes them bloom. The lightly blanched asparagus is the perfect crisp-tender foil to the creamy beans, and the tang of the pepperoncini, lemon, and garlic gives the main ingredients a unifying brightness. I make these to serve in a small bowl with other snacks or to toss in salads when I don't have a ton of other vegetables on hand. I also top toasts with them for a quick crostini or bruschetta. SERVES 6 TO 8

Bring a medium pot of salted water to a boil. Add the asparagus spears and blanch, removing them as soon as they turn bright green and the water has returned to a boil. Run the asparagus under cold water to stop the cooking process and drain.

Put the asparagus and butter beans in a large bowl and add the olive oil, shallot, lemon zest and juice, garlic, pepperoncini, oregano, and red pepper flakes. Stir gently to combine. Add the vinegar and season with salt and black pepper—you want a pretty robust marinade so the flavors penetrate the beans.

Transfer the bean mixture to a lidded jar (24 to 32 ounces) and put in the fridge for at least 2 hours and up to overnight, if possible. Keep in mind the beans will absorb the flavors as they sit, so give the jar a gentle shake now and then and taste along the way, adjusting the seasoning if you think it's missing something. Serve straight from the jar or in small dishes with toothpicks for spearing.

Potted Salmon, Smoked and Fresh

2½ cups water

1 cup dry white wine

4 ounces salmon fillet, skinned

Sea salt

4 tablespoons unsalted butter, at room temperature

1 medium shallot, finely minced

1 tablespoon crème fraîche or clotted cream

4 ounces smoked salmon

Juice of ½ lemon

Pinch of freshly ground black pepper

Platters and boards are enticing because they offer a bounty of flavors and textures all at once, like when we first see the presents under the tree at Christmas. There's so much to delight: where do we start, what makes us swoon? Half the fun of grazing is the element of surprise, which this potted salmon has. The nifty part of this recipe is the combination of fresh and smoked salmon—together you end up with a sweet yet bold, smoky but subtle pâté. I surround the jar with a medley of fresh vegetables and a smattering of crackers or toasts when it's an evening thing, but this recipe also translates beautifully to earlier in the day—put out a few little bowls filled with capers, minced red onion, and some fresh dill along with some jammy soft-boiled eggs. Even a few mini bagels on the side wouldn't be wrong. SERVES 4 TO 6

In a medium saucepan, bring the water and wine to a simmer over medium-high heat. Sprinkle the salmon fillet with salt, reduce the heat to medium, and add the fish to the liquid (it should just barely cover the fish). Cook, keeping the liquid at a gentle simmer, until the fish flakes with a fork and is light pink, 5 to 7 minutes. Remove the salmon from the pan and set aside.

Meanwhile, in a small sauté pan, melt 1 tablespoon of the butter and cook the shallot until just tender and fragrant but not coloring, about 2 minutes. Remove from the heat and set aside.

In a medium bowl, combine 2 tablespoons of the butter with the crème fraîche. Using a silicone spatula, whip the mixture until it's well blended and thickened. Use a fork to flake the poached salmon into chunks and add it to the bowl. Chop the smoked salmon into small pieces and add to the bowl along with the sautéed shallots. Stir aggressively to combine everything and break up the poached salmon into bite-size pieces. Season the mixture with the lemon juice and salt and pepper to taste.

In a small saucepan, melt the remaining 1 tablespoon butter over low heat. Transfer the salmon mixture to a lidded jar (12 to 14 ounces), smooth the top, and pour the melted butter over the salmon to seal it. Place in the fridge to chill until ready to serve; it will keep up to 3 days in the fridge.

Fig and Balsamic Jam

1 pound fresh figs (about 18), stemmed and halved

2 tablespoons honey, plus more as needed

¼ cup water

1 tablespoon freshly squeezed lemon juice, plus more as needed

½ tablespoon balsamic vinegar, plus more as needed

I'm a sucker for fresh figs in any preparation, but one of the purest ways to eat figs (beyond the obvious, right off the tree) is to cook them down quickly into a jam. And because figs are seasonal, it's hard to not overbuy them when they're available—as if stocking up on something perishable makes any sense at all. But that's what I usually do. I find myself with far more fresh figs than can be eaten before they start to go soft and so I make this simple jam. Often more than once a season. With very little added sweetener—just a bit of honey, which mimics the fig's own honeyed flavor—this jam benefits from a kiss of acid in the form of lemon and some good-quality balsamic. A slice of brioche bread or a good dollop with a creamy cheese and it's as close to bottling fresh figs as I've found.

SERVES 6 TO 8

In a medium saucepan, combine the figs, honey, water, and lemon juice over medium-high heat. Bring the mixture to a boil, lower the heat to medium-low, and cook, stirring occasionally, until the figs are very tender and the skins are beginning to fall apart, about 20 minutes.

Carefully transfer the cooked figs to the bowl of a food processor and pulse until pureed. Add the balsamic vinegar and pulse again to combine. Taste the jam and adjust the flavoring—honey, lemon, or vinegar—as you think is needed. Transfer the jam to a jar (16 to 24 ounces) and keep in the fridge until ready to serve. Store leftover jam in an airtight container in the fridge for up to 1 week.

Also pictured: Rhubarb and Blood Orange Compote (page 89)

Apple-Honey Fruit Paste

1½ pounds tart apples (such as Pippin, Granny Smith, or similar), peeled and roughly chopped

½ cup water

½ cup honey

2 tablespoons freshly squeezed lemon juice

Membrillo is a Spanish delicacy, a dense jam or "cheese" made from quince that you usually find in little tubs in gourmet shops. This is not a mebrillo, but it's a nod the same idea—a fruit paste full of sweetness and tang that can be served with cheese and charcuterie or just smeared on toast. The beauty of this recipe, besides how spare it is, is that it doesn't rely on quince, which can be hard to come by. Instead, by using tart apples, this is a treat that can be made all year long. The addition of honey (as opposed to sugar) gives this a caramelly, earthy flavor resonate of autumn. SERVES 4 TO 6

In a large saucepan, combine the apples with the water and bring to a boil. Reduce the heat the medium and simmer the apples until they're very tender, about 15 minutes.

Drain the apples and transfer them to the bowl of a food processor. Puree until you have a very smooth mixture, scraping down the sides of the bowl as needed, 1 to 2 minutes.

Transfer the pureed fruit back to the saucepan over medium-low heat. Stir in the honey and lemon juice. When the fruit is hot and begins to bubble, lower the heat to low and cook, stirring frequently, for 10 minutes. Once the apples begin to dry out and are just sticking to the pan, begin stirring constantly to keep them from scorching. The apple mixture will begin to reduce significantly and little reddish speckles will appear. When the mixture is almost totally dry and pulls away from the bottom in a cohesive mass, 25 to 30 minutes, remove from the heat.

At this point you can transfer the paste to a lidded jar (8 to 12 ounces) or, if you want a sliceable loaf, like a mebrillo, transfer it to a shallow glass storage container. Let the paste sit at room temperature until cool, then transfer to the fridge to fully set before serving, about 2 hours. Store leftover apple-honey paste in an airtight container in the fridge for up to 1 week.

Rhubarb and
Blood Orange Compote

1 pound rhubarb,
trimmed and cut
into ½-inch pieces

½ cup sugar

2 tablespoons water

Juice of 1 blood orange

Rhubarb is a vegetable (a member of the buckwheat family to be precise), but because of its fruity-tart flavor, it's easily brought around to the sweeter side with a touch of sugar or honey and is frequently put to good use in desserts. For those of us who favor savory over sweet, rhubarb is the perfect way to meet in the middle when it comes to tarts, pies, and, of course, jams and compotes. One of the biggest problems I have with most jams and the like is that they are often laden with so much sugar as to render their fruit flavor almost undetectable. But with rhubarb, when treated properly, you can balance out the tartness with just a hint of sugar and round out the slightly sour notes by adding a generous dose of citrus juice. I choose blood oranges here specifically, not simply because they enhance the rosy color of the rhubarb, but because they also add a gentle fruity note that's unexpected but delicious (akin to what happens when you mix berries with rhubarb). This easy compote can be spooned on yogurt and granola, over ice cream, spread on toast, or eaten simply solo out of a bowl. And if you're a gardener, I suggest you plant rhubarb; one or two plants will give you plenty, and most delightfully, they're perennials, so they will come back every year largely untended. **SERVES 6 TO 8**

In a large saucepan, combine the rhubarb, sugar, water, and orange juice over medium heat. Bring the mixture to a simmer and cook, stirring occasionally, until the sugar fully dissolves and the rhubarb begins to fall apart. Continue cooking the compote until it's thickened, about 20 minutes.

Taste the compote and, if it's too tart for you, add a bit more sugar and continue cooking until it's fully dissolved. When you're satisfied with the sweetness, transfer to a lidded jar (16 to 24 ounces) and serve either chilled or at room temperature. Store leftover compote in an airtight container in the fridge for up to 2 weeks.

NAPKINS ONLY

A FRIEND ONCE TOLD ME THAT HANDS WERE THE CHEF'S BEST TOOL. I took this to heart, as at the moment she said it, I was holding a cold, somewhat sticky, cobwebbed piece of caul fat, which I was trying to artfully drape over a raw chicken breast so that the netting of the fat made a tidy lace pattern over the poultry (I was only partially succeeding). My success with this task aside, she was right. Hands are crucial to the cook and, I'd argue, just as essential to the eater.

Eating with one's hands is, while obviously not appropriate in many situations, highly practical and lots of fun in others. And, while I'm not a fan of the term "finger food," that is basically what I'm talking about here: food that can be picked up without a fork or a spoon, that doesn't require a knife, and that really relies only on a good appetite. You will want napkins, though.

I think I'm a bit prone to eating with my hands for two reasons. First, as a cook, tasting things with your fingers is kind of just natural (I mean, not in a professional kitchen where you would of course use a spoon, but at home). You dip your finger into the lemon curd to see if it needs more acid, you grab a blanched bean to make sure it really is crisp-tender, and you peel off a bit of the chicken skin because it's delicious, crispy chicken skin, for God's sake. But the other reason I eat with my hands is that it adds another sensory aspect to eating in general. Not only do you smell and taste the food, but when you eat with your hands, you feel it as well. Batty as it sounds, there is something sensual about food you pick up directly and feed yourself (or someone else), nothing else needed.

For anyone who thinks the idea of eating with your hands is unsavory, I ask you to consider the french fry. French fries, like so many other perfect foods, are meant to be eaten by hand. They actually don't taste as good if you use a fork, in my opinion. But the same goes for many foods; think of charcuterie and cheese boards, tacos, pizza, toast, cookies, and potato chips. And then there's Ethiopian cuisine, which is eaten (as I understand it) almost entirely with the hands. I've even been known to have my way with a bit of salad using only my fingers as utensils when the mood strikes.

Which is all a way of saying that the recipes in this chapter are specifically intended to be eaten and enjoyed sans silverware. Some are truly tiny bite-size snacks while others are moderately more substantial, enough for sharing if you don't mind tearing—napkins only, no forks or knives allowed.

Tater Tots with Crème Fraîche and Caviar

6 large russet potatoes

3 tablespoons potato starch

1½ teaspoons sea salt, plus more as needed

3 to 4 sprigs fresh rosemary, leaves picked and finely minced

Neutral oil (such as vegetable), for frying

Caviar or salmon roe for serving

Crème fraîche or sour cream for serving

I know these might sound silly, included with a lineup like pâté and gougères, but they're actually a sophisticated snack when made by hand. In truth, these homemade tater tots have more in common with the classic French croquettes than the bagged tots found in the frozen food section that most of us are familiar with. By using two different cooking methods for the potatoes—half the blend is dry and fluffy while the other half is moist and textured—the final product has a tender, delicate feel while still maintaining a toothsome bite and a crispy outer crunch. I like to serve these with crème fraîche or sour cream and caviar (the tot is a fun twist on the buckwheat blini) for a high-brow/low-brow accompaniment to a bottle of fizz. But you can also keep it simple and serve them solo, as the rosemary gives them enough flavor to stand alone (no ketchup needed). And because you can freeze them and fry them straight out of the freezer, having a few extra around make a perfect side dish as well. SERVES 6 TO 8

Set an oven rack to the middle position and preheat the oven to 400°F.

Using a small sharp knife, stab 3 of the potatoes all over, 6 to 8 times each. Place these potatoes on the rack and bake until soft, 45 minutes to 1 hour.

Meanwhile, put the remaining 3 potatoes in a large pot of salted water and bring to a boil. Cook the potatoes until a knife just pierces the center, 20 to 25 minutes. Drain and, when cool enough to handle, peel all the potatoes.

Using a ricer, press the baked potatoes through the grates or holes into a large bowl. Finely chop the parboiled potatoes until they are about the size of small peas; you want them to have some texture in contrast to the riced potatoes. Add the finely chopped potatoes to the bowl along with the potato starch, sea salt, and rosemary. Using your hands, gently mix everything together, being careful not to overblend.

(recipe continues)

Line a baking sheet with parchment paper. Form the potato mixture into 1-inch logs (aka tots), pressing them firmly enough so they hold their shape. Once all the tots have been formed, you have two choices: You can deep-fry the tots immediately or you can freeze them uncooked to fry later. If you want to fry them at a later time, use a baking sheet that will fit in your freezer and arrange them close together but not touching. Freeze until firm, about 2 hours, and then transfer them to airtight containers in the freezer until you're ready to cook—they can go straight from frozen into the hot oil.

If you want to cook the tots now, line a baking sheet with paper towels.

Pour 4 inches of oil into a large deep pot. Heat the oil over medium heat, bringing it to 350°F (use a candy thermometer and try not to let the temperature get above 375°F). Add the tots to the pot in small batches (if you overcrowd the pan, you'll bring the temperature down and they won't cook evenly). Let the tots fry until they are a gorgeous amber color, 6 to 8 minutes, then use a slotted spoon or spider to transfer them to the paper towel–lined baking sheet to cool. Sprinkle immediately with sea salt. You can serve immediately with a small dish of caviar or roe and crème fraîche or sour cream, or reheat the tater tots in a 300°F oven within a couple of hours.

Gruyère Gougères

1 cup water

3 tablespoons unsalted butter

1 teaspoon sea salt

1 cup (140 grams) all-purpose flour

4 large eggs

½ teaspoon freshly ground black pepper, or to taste

3½ ounces Gruyère cheese, grated

Pâte à choux, the base of gougères, employs a very traditional technique that doesn't differ much from recipe to recipe; the main ingredients are water, butter, flour, and eggs, and it's made on the stovetop before being baked. What I've found makes this version special is the bite of black pepper and the abundance of cheese. It's derived from a New Year's Eve recipe by Judy Rogers of Zuni Café fame and barely touched except to up the cheese quotient—nearly doubled, in fact—and to cook the puffs at a slightly higher temperature for a really crisp exterior. (Full disclosure: These tweaks were a happy accident. I grated too much cheese and decided instead of leaving a small bag of shredded Gruyère sulking in the cheese drawer, I'd dump it all into the pan.) The result is a delicate, almost brittle crust surrounding a tender inner custard; the perfect little airy bites to serve with a bottle of dry Champagne. That said, I think they're too good to save for just once a year, so I make these and freeze them (piped but not yet baked) to have on hand all the time. They can go straight from the freezer into the oven. SERVES 4 TO 6

Preheat the oven to 425°F. Line two baking sheets with parchment paper and set aside (if you plan to make these ahead and freeze to bake later, be sure to prepare baking sheets that will fit in your freezer).

In a medium saucepan, combine the water, butter, and salt and cook over medium heat until the butter has melted and the mixture is just simmering. Add the flour and cook, stirring constantly with a wooden spoon, until it's all combined and you have a cohesive mass of dough in the pan. Lower the heat to low and keep mixing the dough and drying it out until it's quite firm, about 5 minutes. Remove from the heat and let cool for a few minutes so you don't cook the eggs when adding them.

Add the eggs one at a time, beating the mixture continuously until they blend in. This takes some real effort and a bit of time. The batter will fight you at first, but it will get easier with each egg as the dough absorbs the liquid and finally become a sticky,

(recipe continues)

spreadable mass. Mix in the pepper and cheese until well combined. (Alternatively, you can transfer the cooled dough to the bowl of a stand mixer and add the eggs, one at a time, using the paddle attachment, if you prefer.)

Use a silicone spatula to transfer the batter to a large pastry bag fitted with a ½-inch (or thereabouts) round tip. At this point you have two options: You can pipe the batter onto the prepared baking sheets and cook them to eat immediately, or you can pipe them onto the baking sheets that will fit in your freezer and freeze the gougères to bake off when your friends arrive so they're crisp and still warm. If you choose to freeze them ahead to bake later, you don't need to cover the baking sheets; simply let the gougères freeze (about 2 hours) and then transfer them to an airtight container and return them to freezer until ready to bake. They can go straight from the freezer into the oven. They can also be frozen once baked and warmed, but I've found freezing them uncooked offers a much nicer result.

To pipe the batter, make an initial ring about 2 inches in diameter and then swirl and raise the tip, leaving a Hershey's Kiss–like peak on top. Bake the gougères until fully puffed and golden brown, 20 to 25 minutes; they should be crisp on the outside and tender and custardy on the inside. Serve warm.

Favas Fritas
with Frizzled Parsley

1 cup dried, peeled
fava beans

Neutral oil (such as
vegetable) for frying

Sea salt

Good handful of
flat-leaf parsley
(15 to 18 stems),
stems intact

These crispy snacks are a revelation. Yes, you can buy very small containers of them now in some fancier markets and they're good. But nothing will prepare you for how much more delicious they are when you make them yourself—and how much more affordable. What you want here are not fresh, canned, or frozen fava beans but the inexpensive dry ones that usually come in plastic bags in the dried bean section of the market. If you can't find them at your local grocery store, you can almost always find them in Hispanic markets or online. And because once you commit to deep-frying—it's just as easy to deep-fry a lot as it is a little—I'd suggest you get a couple of bags so you can amortize your oil, as I think you'll find them so addictive you'll want to make them somewhat regularly. I add the fried parsley (it takes mere seconds to cook once the oil is hot and the favas are cooling) because it transforms these from a shy little snack to a vibrant, eye-catching delicacy of amber-toned beans flecked with forest-green leafy bits. Salty, crunchy, and creamy (they are beans, after all), this recipe requires three things of you: to get over any fear you have of using a candy thermometer (don't fret—it's just like any other thermometer), to be attentive to the heat (keep it hovering around 350°F and you'll be fine), and to be careful with the hot oil (use pot holders and let the phone ring—they'll call back). I know frying is a bit of a to-do—it isn't something I do a ton of at home either—but some recipes are worth the extra care and cleanup, and this is definitely one of them. Last thought: Oil can be used a couple of times within a month or so. Once your pot of oil is completely cool, funnel it back into an empty container and use that as an excuse to make another batch soon. Or try the Tater Tots with Caviar and Crème Fraîche on page 96, which also require deep-frying (and are also worth it). **SERVES 6 TO 8**

Line a baking sheet with paper towels and set aside.

In a medium bowl, soak the beans in enough cold water to cover for at least 12 hours or overnight. Drain, rinse, and pat the beans dry—you don't want them to splatter when frying.

(recipe continues)

Pour 4 inches of oil into a deep saucepan and heat the oil over medium heat, bringing it to 350°F (use a candy thermometer and try not to let the temperature get above 375°F). Add the fava beans and fry until they are a rich golden brown, 6 to 7 minutes. Use a slotted spoon or spider to transfer them to the prepared baking sheet and sprinkle immediately with sea salt. Let cool.

While the oil is still hot, carefully add the parsley to the pan and fry until it turns dark green and frizzles in the oil, about 30 seconds. Remove the parsley from the hot oil with a slotted spoon or spider and transfer it to the baking sheet to drain alongside the favas. When everything is cool, crumble the fried parsley over the favas, transfer to a serving bowl, and toss to combine. Serve immediately. Store leftover favas in an airtight container at room temperature for up to 2 weeks.

Leek and Carbonara Quichettes

½ cup (112 grams) cold unsalted butter, cut into ½-inch pieces

1¼ cups (175 grams) all-purpose flour

¼ teaspoon sea salt, plus more as needed

¼ to ½ cup ice water

2 ounces pancetta, diced

1 leek, white parts, finely chopped

2 large eggs

½ cup whole milk

½ cup heavy cream

Freshly ground black pepper

½ cup finely grated Parmesan

2 ounces spaghetti, cooked al dente per package directions

Carbonara, that classic combination of pancetta, eggs, cheese, and black pepper, is one of my favorite pastas. I find the way the smoky, creamy, salty spiciness gets all tangled up in the spaghetti beguiling; it's one of those dishes that makes even the bumpiest of days a bit smoother—the pasta equivalent of chicken soup. And quiche isn't dissimilar; flaky piecrust replaces pasta as the starch, but the eggs, cream, and cheese are all there, often with bacon and leeks to boot. Which is why blending these two soul-soothing dishes into one just seemed like a good idea. It may sound decadent, but the texture of the spaghetti gives the custard a welcome bite, and the richness of the butter crust elevates its status to true comfort food. Break these into quarters for truly small bites, or serve one quichette per person for a slightly larger snacking event. MAKES 6 QUICHETTES

To make the pastry: In the bowl of a food processor, pulse the butter, flour, and salt until the mixture resembles coarse meal (about ten pulses). Slowly add ¼ cup of the ice water and continue to pulse until the mixture begins to come together. If the dough is too dry, add more water a tablespoon at a time and pulse again but try not to overwork it. Transfer the dough to a lightly floured work surface and bring it all together with your hands, kneading once or twice until it forms a rough ball—you should see patches of butter in places for a flaky crust. Form the dough into a 1-inch-thick disk, wrap in plastic wrap, and refrigerate for at least 30 minutes.

Remove the dough from the fridge. Dust a clean work surface with flour, unwrap the disk, and use a rolling pin to roll it into a 15 by 10-inch rectangle. Cut the dough into six squares, rolling them a bit thinner if necessary to fit the pans. Press the dough evenly into the bottom and up the sides of six 4-inch tart pans. Trim the edges and prick the bottom of the crust lightly with a fork. Freeze or chill the tarts for at least 30 minutes.

Meanwhile, line a plate with paper towels. In a large saucepan, cook the diced pancetta over medium heat until the fat has rendered

(recipe continues)

and the meat is brown but not crispy, about 5 minutes. Use a slotted spoon to remove the pancetta to drain on paper towels. Lower the heat to medium-low and add the chopped leeks. Cook the leeks in the pancetta fat until they are very tender, about 8 minutes, sprinkling with a bit of salt as you go. When the leeks are soft but not coloring, remove them from the heat.

Preheat the oven to 375°F.

While the oven is heating, make the custard: In a medium bowl, whisk together the eggs, milk, and cream and season with salt and a generous amount of black pepper. Fold in the Parmesan and stir again, then add the cooked pancetta and leeks along with the prepared spaghetti.

Remove the chilled crust shells from the freezer and place a piece of foil inside each one, lining the foil up against the edges. Fill the foil-lined shells with pie weights or dry beans to keep the bottoms from puffing up and the edges from sliding down. Transfer the tart pans to a baking sheet and cook until just beginning to color on the edges, 10 to 12 minutes. Remove the shells from the oven, then carefully remove the foil and the weights from the pans. Return the tart shells to the oven until the bottom crusts look dry, 3 to 5 minutes. Remove the tart shells from the oven and lower the oven temperature to 350°F.

Divide the carbonara custard mixture evenly among the tart shells, being careful not to fill them more than two-thirds of the way. Bake until the custard is set, 20 to 25 minutes. Serve hot or at room temperature.

Bacon, Sweet Onion, and Apple Tarts

1 cup (140 grams) all-purpose flour, plus more for the work surface

10 tablespoons (140 grams) unsalted butter, cut into ¼-inch pieces

¼ teaspoon sea salt, plus more as needed

4 to 5 tablespoons ice water

2 slices thick-cut bacon, cut into ¼-inch pieces

1 sweet onion (such as Vidalia), thinly sliced into half-moons

A few sprigs thyme, leaves picked

Extra-virgin olive oil, as needed

Freshly ground black pepper

1 tart apple (such as Pippin or Granny Smith), very thinly sliced

There are certain cheats in the kitchen that I'm totally comfortable with; canned beans and prewashed arugula both make my life easier, and I have no shame in admitting it. But there are other shortcuts that I object to, premade pie dough and puff pastry being among them. I realize that making your own dough takes some time and requires a bit of effort, but it's always worth it as no packaged dough will ever be as flaky, buttery, and delicious as a good homemade one. And here's the thing: Making good homemade pastry isn't a talent doled out at birth. It's a matter of following directions and keeping your dough properly chilled at every stage. Now having said all that, this "rough puff pastry" recipe is really a bit of a cheat as you don't have to refrigerate it with every fold of the dough. Instead, you work quickly and fold it a few times right at the beginning, so it takes only about a half hour to make instead of the more traditional few hours. If you've never made your own puff pastry, I implore you to try. I turned my friend Andi (someone who self-identifies as "not a cook") on to this technique and she's been turning out gorgeous fruit tarts for years now. Here I top the pastry with caramelized sweet onions, tart apples, bacon, and fresh thyme, but you can easily ditch the bacon for a vegetarian option, swap in pears for the apples, or have your way with the toppings based on what you've got in the fridge. Just promise to make your own pastry. **MAKES 4 TARTS**

To make the pastry: Put the flour, butter, and ¼ teaspoon sea salt in a large bowl. Using your fingers, press the butter into the flour until it resembles relatively even coarse meal and most of the flour has been integrated into the butter. Make a well in the center of the bowl and pour 4 tablespoons of the ice water into the flour mixture. Knead the dough gently until it just comes together, adding another tablespoon of water if needed; don't overwork it. You want to see some larger pieces of butter still in the mix (this is the sign of a flaky crust).

Lightly flour your work surface and your rolling pin and turn out the dough. Roll out the dough into a 12 by 6-inch rectangle. Use a bit more flour as needed to keep the dough from sticking, but try not to

(recipe continues)

add too much as this will dry out your dough. Fold the top third of the dough into the center and then fold the bottom third up over that, as if you were folding a letter. Turn the dough 45 degrees and roll it into a 12-inch rectangle again. Repeat the folds and this rolling two more times for a total of four folds; by the time you're done, your dough should look like a very tidy little rectangle. Transfer the dough to a lightly floured plate, cover with plastic wrap, and put it in the fridge to chill for at least 1 hour.

Meanwhile, line a plate with paper towels. In a large frying pan, cook the chopped bacon over medium-high heat until the fat is rendered and the meat is cooked but not crispy, about 5 minutes. Transfer the bacon to the prepared plate to drain and set aside. Add the sliced onion and thyme to the bacon fat and cook over medium heat until the onion begins to soften, about 10 minutes. If the pan seems too dry, add a tablespoon or so of olive oil. Season the onion with salt and pepper and lower the heat to medium-low. Continue cooking, stirring frequently, until the onion begins to color, another 10 minutes or so, then add the sliced apple. Cook for another couple of minutes or until the apple just starts to wilt in the fat. When the onion is very tender and golden and the apple has softened, remove the pan from the heat and let cool.

Preheat the oven to 400°F. Line a baking sheet with parchment paper.

Take the pastry from the fridge and let sit for 5 to 10 minutes on the counter while the oven preheats. When the dough is soft enough to roll out, sprinkle your surface lightly with flour and roll the dough into a large square about 1/4 inch thick, then cut the dough into four roughly shaped squares and roll them out again until they're about 1/8 inch thick and 8 inches in diameter. Place the squares on the prepared baking sheet and lightly prick them all over with a fork.

Spread a few tablespoons of the onion-apple mixture over each piece of dough, leaving a good 1-inch border and sprinkle each with a quarter of the bacon. Fold up the edges of the dough and press firmly on the seams to seal the sides and corners. Transfer the baking sheet to the oven and bake until the crust is golden brown, 20 to 25 minutes. Remove from the oven and serve hot or at room temperature.

Jammy Eggs
with Fried Shallots

6 medium shallots

1 cup extra-virgin olive oil

Sea salt

6 large eggs

Freshly ground black pepper

There are many different schools of thought when it comes to the most exacting method for the perfect jammy egg. This is mine, and while I've tried multiple other approaches, I find this is the one that works most reliably and simply. With this method there's no putting eggs in cold water and then bringing them to a boil before you start the clock, and there's no prepping an ice bath to have at the ready, the first which I find adds too much variability and the second which I just never can be bothered with. And while it sounds like a ridiculously simple preparation, the addition of fried shallots to the eggs is revelatory, as the crispy, salty onions counterbalance the tender, creamy egg—it's a lot of savory flavor in just a couple of bites. Serve these with some fresh veg, smoked fish, a pâté, with toasts or crackers, or even just by themselves. **MAKES 12 EGG HALVES**

Line a plate with paper towels. Peel the shallots and slice them into very thin rings, either using a very sharp knife or a mandoline. In a small saucepan, heat the olive oil over medium-high heat. Add the shallots and lower the heat to medium-low. Cook the shallots, stirring frequently, until they begin to turn golden and then brown, about 15 minutes. Keep a close eye on them as they go quickly in the last few minutes, and you don't want them to burn. When the shallots are a rich brown color, use a slotted spoon to transfer them to the prepared plate to cool; sprinkle immediately with salt. Reserve the shallot oil for a vinaigrette later.

Bring a medium saucepan of water to a boil. Carefully lower the eggs into the boiling water and set your timer for 6 minutes, taking care to keep the water at a constant bubble. Remove the eggs from the water when the timer goes off and immediately run them under cold water for about a minute to help stop the cooking. Transfer them immediately to the fridge.

Once the eggs have cooled, peel them (doing this under water helps the shell come off easily) and cut them in half. The yolks will be just set. Sprinkle with pepper and the fried shallots to serve.

Sea Cakes with Ponzu Dipping Sauce

8 medium shrimp, peeled, tails removed, and deveined

4 medium sea scallops, side muscle removed

1 teaspoon nam pla (fish sauce)

½ pound fresh lump crabmeat, picked over for random shells

1 large egg

4 green onions, white and green parts, finely chopped

Small handful of cilantro (about 6 stems), leaves picked and finely chopped

1 fresh chile, preferably Thai, finely chopped

1 teaspoon grated peeled fresh ginger

Sea salt and freshly ground black pepper

¼ cup bread crumbs, preferably fresh, plus more as needed

About ½ cup all-purpose flour for dredging

Vegetable or olive oil for frying

Ponzu sauce for serving

Lime wedges for serving

I call these "sea cakes" because they rely on shrimp, scallops, and crab—so instead of the taste of a singular shellfish, you really do get a very full oceanic flavor from what are quite small bites. The neat thing here is how the shrimp and scallops are pureed to work as binders; they make a sort of paste that helps hold everything together. Also, unlike a lot of crab cakes that are woefully light on crab and heavy on bread crumbs or crackers, these are mostly shellfish with just enough of everything else to add texture. And they come together very quickly; a fast blitz in the bowl of a food processor for the shrimp and scallops and then a few turns in a bowl and you're ready to cook (if you have the time, a short stint in the fridge after you form them helps them hold their shape but it's not necessary). And don't worry about making these into perfect little cakes; you don't want to compress them too much. They should have an organic look to them, like something that might come from the sea. **SERVES 4 TO 6**

In the bowl of a food processor, pulse the shrimp and scallops until you have a relatively smooth paste. Transfer the paste to a large bowl and add the nam pla, crab, egg, green onions, cilantro, chile, ginger, and salt and pepper. Mix to combine well and then add the bread crumbs to tighten the mixture. If it seems a bit wet, add an extra tablespoon of the crumbs—you want it stiff enough to hold its form. If you have the time, put the bowl in the fridge for half an hour or more, as it'll be easier to work with when chilled.

When you're ready to cook, put the flour into a shallow dish and season it well with salt and pepper.

Set a large skillet over medium-high heat and add enough oil to generously coat the bottom of the pan. Form the seafood mixture into 1-inch-thick patties about 2 inches in diameter. Dredge each patty in the flour. Working in batches so as not to overcrowd the pan, carefully add the cakes to the shimmering oil. Cook, adjusting the heat and adding more oil as necessary, until the cakes are golden brown and release easily. Gently flip the cakes and cook until the second side is nicely browned, about 5 minutes total. Serve immediately with the ponzu and lime wedges.

Chapter 4

IN BOWLS

HISTORICALLY, I DON'T DO DIPS. I love smears, spreads, salsas, and slathers, but dips, at least in name, are not okay with me. The reason I cannot abide the notion of dips, or at least the connotations that come to mind when someone says, "I'll bring the dip," is simple: I grew up in the 1970s.

Some might glamorize that time as the decade of disco and bell-bottoms, but when I think of the '70s, what jumps to mind is the culinary travesty known as dip, when a packet of onion soup was merrily stirred into a pint of sour cream and seven layers were stacked high in Pyrex dishes. Nothing about these concoctions holds the least appeal, and unfortunately, their mere existence has tainted an entire category of food for me. But pass me a good smear, spread, or salsa, a bowl of something smooth and savory, and I'm bewitched.

What separates a smear or a spread from the dreaded dip is integrity, meaning the ingredients are whole and generally need little added fat (read: sour cream, cream cheese, or mayonnaise) to be delicious. The point of a good spread or smear (okay, *dip*) is to taste the main ingredients in their purest form, enhanced delicately and thoughtfully by a few other discrete ingredients.

I spent years avoiding dips at parties and on holidays, turning a blind eye to the dishes of ambiguous goo surrounded by chips and celery sticks and, in turn, never bothered to make them either. That was until I discovered hummus. Not the packaged kind you find in tubs in the refrigerated section of the market, but the kind that you get at a good Middle Eastern restaurant on the Edgeware Road in London. Which is exactly where I first tasted authentic hummus and where my prejudice against dips on a whole started to abate.

While living briefly in London right after college, a friend, one who had traveled far more extensively than I had and who was far more worldly in terms of food than I was, took me to a Lebanese restaurant. It was there, among the falafel and the fattoush, that I met my first bowl of creamy, swirly, lighter-than-air, olive oil–laced, cumin-kissed, pureed chickpeas, a dip that bore absolutely no resemblance to the cream-and-garlic-powder-powered dishes I'd known. Six thousand miles from home and I finally discovered what all the fuss was about. This was what all those other dips were aiming for—and missing wildly.

From that first bowl of hummus on, my aversion to dips has been more a matter of semantics than anything else. Since that lunch eons ago, I've played with all kinds of ingredients to create smears and spreads of all sorts. One of my greatest successes is a ten-minute Artichoke and Green Olive Tapenade (page 120) that relies on little more than artichokes, olives, and capers to dazzle. But some of my favorites are bean-based (such as hummus) because the humble legume purees into creamy, clingy mixtures just right for scooping. With recipes like these, you can have fun and experiment without the risk of going too far astray. In fact, a close friend recently admitted to me that she makes my Butter Beans with Asparagus (sans the asparagus) on page 84 and instead of serving them whole as I do, she pulses them in the bowl of a food processor so that the butter beans, pepperoncini, and marinade all become one loose but lovely bowl of goodness to serve with raw veg. Something I've never thought to try but plan to, because, why not? The flavors are all there just waiting to be smoothed out and slathered.

One of the best things about dips is that they open you up to new worlds of flavor with a minimal amount of effort. Whether it's an Egyptian-inspired bessara or an Oaxacan-style salsa, a broccoli rabe puree or a trout-topped avocado spread, the ideal dip reveals its essential flavors boldly and readily, without too much tinkering on the part of the cook. And that's good, because what I want in a bowl of something spreadable is simplicity in the making and complexity in the taste. I want to be able to sauté a couple of vegetables together or puree a few fresh ingredients (hold the sour cream, please) and create something wonderful to snack on. I hope that's what you'll find here: bowls of delicious spreads, salsas, smears, or (I reluctantly admit) what should probably just be called dips.

Artichoke and Green Olive Tapenade

One 14-ounce can artichoke hearts, drained

1 cup pitted Cerignola, Castelvetrano, or Frescatrano green olives

1 tablespoon capers (in brine, not salt)

1 small or ½ large garlic clove

¼ to ⅓ cup extra-virgin olive oil

Juice of ½ lemon, plus more as needed

Sea salt and freshly ground black pepper

Every cook I know has a couple of parlor tricks they hold in reserve for emergencies, be it an unexpected guest, a quick fix to replace a kitchen fail, or just an easy out after a long day. A "Look, no hands!" sort of maneuver. These old reliables aren't something to be ashamed of, yet I always feel secretly like I'm cheating with this one, because it is just too easy and the ingredients are things I almost always have on hand. I'm also slightly embarrassed by it, because while I love artichokes with a deep and abiding passion, the ones in cans are pretty sad as a rule and usually bear no resemblance to their fresh cousins. That said, they work here because what you want is that soft consistency and slightly briny flavor as a complement to the rich, meaty olives. When someone gives you ten minutes' notice before dropping by, this dip can save you. Serve this lifesaver with whatever crackers or toasts you have on hand. SERVES 4 TO 6

In the bowl of a food processor, blitz the artichokes, olives, capers, and garlic until chunky, 20 to 30 seconds.

Drizzle ¼ cup of olive oil into the mix and add the lemon juice. Process until the mixture is relatively smooth but not a full puree—you want the final tapenade to have some structure.

Taste and season with salt and pepper as needed and more lemon juice as well. If the mixture is too thick or chunky for your taste, add a bit more olive oil and pulse again. Transfer the mixture to a bowl and chill until ready to serve.

Arugula, White Bean, and Roasted Garlic Smear

1 garlic head

1 tablespoon extra-virgin olive oil, plus ¼ cup

One 14-ounce can cannellini beans, rinsed and drained, (or 2 cups cooked)

2 good handfuls of baby arugula (about 2 ounces)

Zest and juice of 1 lemon

Sea salt and freshly ground black pepper

For years I've made a very simple white bean dip that consists of little more than beans, garlic, rosemary, and lemon. And, while I'm not one to mess with traditional hummus (meaning, I refuse to add beets, chocolate, or pumpkin pie spice, no matter how good you tell me it may be), I have no issue messing around with white beans. White beans, by which I mean cannellini, navy, or butter beans, provide a rich, creamy backdrop that lets other, more vibrant flavors pop. With this in mind, to create a white bean concoction that's a little brighter and a little richer than my old standby, I've swapped roasted garlic for raw (yes, it requires a bit more effort and time on the cook's part, but the softer, less fiery, and more earthy result is worth it). And gravitating to one of my favorite greens (arugula) over the more obvious choice of spinach, gives this dip a fresh, peppery, and verdant bite. SERVES 4 TO 6

Preheat the oven to 400°F. Cut the top off the garlic head to expose the flesh of the cloves. Place the head in the center of a piece of aluminum foil, drizzle the top of the garlic with about a tablespoon of olive oil, just enough to moisten it, and then bundle the garlic in the foil so it's completely enclosed. Put the garlic on a baking sheet and roast until it's fragrant and very soft, 45 minutes. To check, carefully open the foil pouch and press on the exposed garlic with a paring knife—if it's still a bit firm, reseal the foil and continue cooking for another 15 minutes or so.

When the garlic is done, let it cool until you can handle it, then squeeze out the flesh of the cloves into a small airtight container. At this point you want to separate out 3 or 4 cloves for the dip and freeze the remainder to use later.

In the bowl of a food processor, puree the beans and roasted garlic cloves until the mixture is coarse. With the machine running, slowly stream in the remaining ¼ cup olive oil. When the mixture is smooth, add the arugula and continue to process until the greens are fully integrated, adding more oil if needed until you have a creamy puree.

Add the lemon zest and half the juice, sprinkle with salt and pepper, then pulse again. Taste the puree and add more arugula, lemon, or salt and pepper as needed.

*Arugula, White Bean, and
Roasted Garlic Smear
(page 121); Fennel Ratatouille
Salsa (page 124); Artichoke
and Green Olive Tapenade
(page 120); and Parmesan
Grissini (page 190)*

Fennel Ratatouille Salsa

1 medium eggplant, cut into ½-inch dice

Sea salt

8 tablespoons extra-virgin olive oil

1 large zucchini, cut into ½-inch dice

1 medium fennel bulb, trimmed, cored, and cut into ¼-inch dice

1 medium sweet onion, cut into ½-inch dice

3 medium garlic cloves, minced

½ teaspoon fennel seeds

¼ teaspoon red pepper flakes

5 plum tomatoes, chopped

3 sprigs oregano, leaves picked

Freshly ground black pepper

12 or more large basil leaves, cut into very thin ribbons

The idea of ratatouille is appealing to me, but the traditional execution—which is reliant on bell peppers—is not. I don't hate the pepper, but I don't love how it tends to overpower other flavors that I like more. To solve my bell pepper issue, I've devised a version of ratatouille that relies heavily on a vegetable I absolutely adore: fennel. I've also gone one step further in mucking about with convention and made this ratatouille into a salsa by dicing everything quite small (the smaller the better, really, but don't drive yourself crazy) and serving it at room temperature. The purists among you may take issue with my tweaks, but a fennel-focused ratatouille salsa is exactly what I want to spoon on toasted bread or to accompany a few thick slices of soppressata. And unless you're truly passionate about bell peppers, I honestly don't think you'll miss them a bit.

SERVES 6 TO 8

Put the eggplant into a colander set over a bowl and lightly sprinkle it with salt, toss to coat, and let it stand for 20 minutes. Discard any liquid that accumulated in the bowl.

In a large saucepan, heat 3 tablespoons of the olive oil over medium heat until it's just shimmering, about 1 minute. Add the eggplant and cook, stirring frequently, until it becomes tender and is beginning to stick to the pan, 5 to 6 minutes. Remove the pan from the heat and transfer the eggplant to a large bowl.

Add 2 more tablespoons of the olive oil to the pan and lower the heat to medium. Add the zucchini, season with salt, and cook, stirring frequently, 5 to 6 minutes. You don't want it to color, just soften. (The zucchini and the eggplant may both stick somewhat to the pan, but don't worry, the fennel and onion will help deglaze it.) Remove the squash from the heat and add it to the bowl with the eggplant.

Add 2 more tablespoons of the olive oil to the same pan set over medium heat. Add the fennel, season with salt, and cook, stirring occasionally, until quite soft and translucent, about 8 minutes. Remove the fennel from the heat and add it to the bowl with the eggplant and zucchini.

Return the pan to the stove again, still over medium heat, and add the remaining 1 tablespoon olive oil. Add the onion and cook, stirring frequently, until it's soft and translucent, about 5 minutes. Add the garlic, fennel seeds, red pepper flakes, and a couple grinds of black pepper and cook for another 1 to 2 minutes, until the aromatics are just fragrant. Add the tomatoes and oregano and cook, stirring occasionally, until the tomatoes begin to break down and release their juices, 5 more minutes. Return the reserved eggplant, zucchini, and fennel mixture to the pan and stir to combine everything well. Lower the heat to low and gently simmer until everything thickens, about 10 minutes. Taste, adjust the salt and black pepper as needed, remove from the heat, and let cool.

When the mixture cools to room temperature, transfer it to an airtight container and refrigerate for at least a couple of hours, preferably overnight, to allow the flavors to meld.

To serve, bring the salsa back to room temperature and stir in the fresh basil.

Also pictured: Middle Eastern–Style Flatbread (page 195)

Bessara
with Harissa

1 cup dried, peeled
fava beans

1 medium garlic clove,
smashed

3 tablespoons
extra-virgin olive oil

Juice of 1 lemon,
or to taste

2 tablespoons harissa

1 teaspoon ground
cumin

½ teaspoon sea salt,
plus more as needed

Pinch of cayenne
of pepper

A few sprigs mint,
flat-leaf parsley,
cilantro, dill, or a
combination, leaves
picked for garnish

Bessara, a traditional Egyptian and North African dip that can also
be thinned into a soup, is a stellar alternative to hummus (and far less
ubiquitous). If you're not familiar with it, bessara is made from fava
beans instead of chickpeas, is creamy and buttery with a bit of heat,
and is often served garnished with fresh herbs and some finely sliced
red onion. My version strays from tradition by adding a good dose of
harissa, which gives it more depth than just cayenne alone. If you've
eaten bessara in places where it's the local specialty, I apologize if the
liberties I've taken seem inauthentic, but give it a try. Served with
Middle Eastern–Style Flatbread (page 195), this may just replace
hummus as your dip of choice. One thing to note: Making the dip
itself is very fast, but you must allow time for soaking dried favas.
SERVES 4 TO 6

Put the beans in a large pot and cover them with at least 3 inches
of cold water. Let them soak for 12 hours or overnight. Drain the
beans and transfer them back to the pot along with 2 quarts of fresh
water. Bring the water to a boil, then reduce the heat to medium, and
simmer the beans until they're tender but not totally falling apart,
30 to 40 minutes. Drain the beans, reserving ½ cup of the cooking
liquid, and transfer the beans to the bowl of a food processor.

Pulse the beans a few times, then add the garlic, olive oil, lemon
juice, harissa, cumin, salt, and cayenne. Puree the mixture until it's
very smooth, adding some of the cooking liquid, a tablespoon at a
time, if it seems too thick. Taste the bessara and adjust the seasoning
as desired. Sprinkle with fresh herbs and serve the dip slightly warm
or at room temperature.

Smashed Avocado with Smoked Trout

2 large avocados, halved and pitted

2 green onions, white and light green parts only, finely sliced

Juice of 1 lemon

Sea salt and freshly ground black pepper

3 to 4 sprigs flat-leaf parsley, leaves picked and roughly chopped

4 ounces smoked trout, flaked

This falls into the "not really a recipe" category of recipes. It's more an assemblage of good ingredients, more about mashing and flaking than actually cooking. But that's okay. Things don't have to be hard to be good, and this is certainly one of those things. Make sure your avocados are ripe and don't be stingy with the trout; you want to get a bit of fish in every bite. I find smoked trout usually comes in 8-ounce packages—it's with the smoked salmon in my market—so I have no hesitancy doubling this recipe if I'm serving a larger group (though the trout also freezes well). **SERVES 4 TO 6**

Scoop out the flesh of the avocados into a medium bowl. With a fork or potato masher, smash the avocado until it's a relatively homogenous consistency with a few larger chunks still visible. Add the green onions and lemon juice and season with salt and pepper. Taste the avocado mixture and adjust the seasoning as needed.

When you're ready to serve, gently fold the parsley into the avocado mixture. Add the flaked trout on top. Serve with toasts, crackers, fresh vegetables, or even chips.

Black Bean Spread
with Pickled Radishes

Pickled Radishes

1 cup distilled white vinegar

1 cup water

¼ cup sugar

1½ tablespoons sea salt, plus more as needed

1 bay leaf, preferably fresh

1 dried red chile

6 medium radishes, trimmed and thinly sliced

½ small red onion, thinly sliced into half-moons

Black Bean Spread

One 15.5-ounce can black beans, rinsed and drained (or 2 cups cooked)

½ bunch of cilantro (12 to 15 stems), leaves picked (some stems are okay too)

½ jalapeño, minced

Juice of 1 lime, plus more as needed

2 teaspoons ground cumin

½ teaspoon chili powder

Pinch of cayenne pepper

Pinch of sea salt

This is a wildly versatile recipe that can be used as a dip for tortilla chips, a topping for tacos, or a spread for Oaxacan-Style Tlayudas (page 175). Serve it warm or at room temperature, skip the radishes if you're in a hurry, and even melt some cheese on top if you feel inclined. Just be sure to keep a can of black beans in your cupboard at all times and you're halfway there. Beyond the beans, it's the fresh cilantro that makes this more than just another bean spread. By blitzing a generous amount of cilantro with the beans, lime, and ground spices, what you get is a remarkably bright, fresh-tasting dip made texturally interesting with the addition of some whole beans folded in at the end. The smooth bean puree is layered with tang and spice, and the whole beans retain their nutty earthiness. I add the radishes because I love how the peppery pickle contrasts with the richness of the dip, but you could easily serve it unadorned and it would still be luscious. SERVES 4 TO 6

To make the pickles: In a small saucepan, combine the vinegar and water over high heat. Add the sugar, salt, bay leaf, and chile and bring to a boil. Stir to make sure the sugar has dissolved, then reduce the heat to medium and add the radishes and onion. Cook until the radishes are slightly translucent and the onion has wilted a bit, about 2 minutes. Remove from the heat and let cool.

To make the black bean spread: Set aside ½ cup of the beans. In the bowl of a food processor, puree the remaining beans, cilantro, jalapeño, lime juice, cumin, chili powder, and cayenne until smooth, adding a bit of water if needed to reach a smooth, creamy consistency. Taste and season with salt and, if needed, more lime juice. Remove the blade from the bowl of the food processor and stir in the reserved whole beans, mashing them a bit as you do so but maintaining some texture. Transfer the spread to a serving bowl.

When the radishes have cooled, transfer them, with as much of the pickling liquid as will fit, to a jar or other lidded container to preserve. Serve the black bean dip and radishes with tortillas chips. Store leftover dip and pickles, separately, in airtight containers in the fridge for up to 1 week.

Charred Corn and Nectarine Relish

1 tablespoon extra-virgin olive oil

4 ears corn, husked

Sea salt and freshly ground black pepper

1 jalapeño, finely chopped

10 to 12 cherry tomatoes, quartered

1 nectarine, pitted and chopped

½ small red onion, finely chopped

6 to 8 basil leaves, finely chopped

Zest and juice of 1 lime

½ teaspoon chili powder

In New England, where I live, summer is punctuated by glorious golden light, fireflies, and farmstands. And come July, these farmstands are laden with piles and piles of freshly picked corn, ears of which I buy by the dozen, as it's such a fleeting treat you just have to bask in its sweetness while you can. At its peak, corn can go in a salad or a salsa raw, but I find that a stint on the grill—just long enough for the kernels to glow sunshine yellow and pick up a bit of black char—enhances the natural sweet flavor and adds a wisp of smokiness and complexity. Mixed with nectarines, this simple relish is basically summer in a jar. You can, of course, substitute peaches, but the tang of nectarines is the perfect contrast to the honeyed corn. Cherry tomatoes, red onion, basil . . . just let Mother Nature do the work here and you have a side salad, a salsa, a topping for tacos, and most definitely, the answer to the proverbial question, "What can I bring?" when you're headed to a picnic or potluck, because it looks as pretty as it tastes. **SERVES 4 TO 6**

Preheat a gas grill to 400°F or, if using a grill pan, set over high heat.

While the grill is heating, lightly oil the corn and season well with salt and pepper. Grill the corn over high heat until beginning to char in spots. Use tongs to flip the corn so they blister on all sides, about 5 minutes total. Remove the corn to a cutting board to cool.

Once cool enough to handle, working with one ear at a time, lay each cob flat on a cutting board. Slice off the first side of kernels, then rotate the ear so the cut side is on the board stabilizing the cob, and continue to cut and rotate. You should have about 3 cups of corn.

Transfer the kernels to a large bowl and stir in the jalapeño, tomatoes, nectarine, onion, and basil. Add the zest and half the lime juice and season with the chili powder, salt, and pepper. Toss well to combine and taste, adding more juice, salt, and pepper as needed. Store leftover relish in an airtight container in the fridge for up to 1 week.

Also pictured: Charred Corn and Nectarine Relish (page 131)

Creamy Tomatillo Salsa

8 medium tomatillos, husked and washed

1 small jalapeño

½ small white onion, roughly chopped

½ bunch of cilantro, (12 to 15 stems), leaves and some stems, plus more as needed

Juice of ½ lime, plus more as needed

Pinch of sea salt and freshly ground black pepper

1 avocado, halved and pitted

Oaxaca, Mexico, has been a fashionable destination for a long time, and rightly so: It's a magical place. I first visited Oaxaca in my early twenties and fell hard for the city and, of course, the food. A few years later, I persuaded my mom to go back with me, and we sought out a cooking class taught by a locally renowned chef. The class followed a morning of shopping at the Central de Abastos. The Abastos is a vast and vibrant food emporium south of the city's zócalo (central square). And whether you're a devotee of Mexican food (as I am), or simply taken with the breadth of produce, the abundance of flavors, and the energy of a bustling marketplace, the Abastos is remarkable. Beyond the vibrating hum of people and the spicy aromas are the pyramids of dried chile peppers, mountains of spices and exotic herbs, and piles of produce, including tomatillos. Tomatillos, which look like small green tomatoes with a husk, have a tart, citrusy flavor and were the central ingredient in the salsa we were making that day in class. The original recipe involved charring all the ingredients over an open flame until they were blistered and blackened for a rich, smoky salsa. Over the years, I've taken some license with this and now add raw tomatillos to brighten up the smokiness, along with an avocado for a bit of body. When I'm feeling lazy, I skip the roasting altogether and just puree the fresh ingredients for something really vibrant. **SERVES 6 TO 8**

Preheat the broiler.

Arrange half the tomatillos and the jalapeño on a baking sheet and broil until beginning to char in spots, about 5 minutes. Flip the tomatillos and pepper so they blister on all sides, another 3 or 4 minutes. Remove from the oven. When cool enough to handle, destem the jalapeño and halve the roasted tomatillos. Halve the remaining fresh tomatillos.

In the bowl of a food processor, combine the roasted tomatillos and jalapeño with the remaining fresh tomatillos, onion, and cilantro and puree until smooth. Add the lime juice and season with salt and pepper. Taste and add more cilantro, lime, or salt and pepper as needed. Add the avocado. Puree until creamy and serve with chips. Store leftovers in an airtight container in the fridge for up to 3 days.

Creamy Broccoli Rabe with Pistachios

1 bunch broccoli rabe, trimmed

1 cup freshly grated Parmesan

½ cup pistachios, plus more for garnish if desired

¼ cup olive oil, plus more as needed

1 cup ricotta cheese

Sea salt and freshly ground black pepper

Imagine you're a long, leafy, floret-laden vegetable full of delicious green, pungent, and slightly bitter flavor. Wouldn't you want to live among those other bright and beautiful veggies that always seem to make their way to the snacking platter—the radishes and snap peas, the asparagus spears and endive leaves? Of course you would. But sadly, you're just a little too tough to love raw, a little too cruciferous to be crudité. What do you do? You get yourself blanched and blitzed, get mixed up with some buttery pistachios, and have your stronger side softened with some creamy ricotta, that's what you do. You stay true to your vegetable heart but reinvent yourself as a dip for those other crunchy vegetables to dive into. You become the center of the plate, the green making all the other vegetables envious. At last, it's all about you, broccoli rabe. **SERVES 4 TO 6**

Bring a large pot of salted water to a boil over high heat. Add the broccoli rabe and cook, stirring, until the water returns to a high boil and the rabe is bright green and tender, 2 to 3 minutes; drain and run the rabe under cool water to slow the cooking process.

When the rabe is cool enough to handle, squeeze the greens over the sink to release as much liquid as you can. Roughly chop the rabe and put it in the bowl of a food processor. Add the Parmesan and pistachios. Pulse the mixture a few times, then, with the machine running, stream in the olive oil. Stop the machine and use a silicone spatula to scrape the edges of the bowl. Run the machine again, adding more oil as needed until you have a smooth, well-combined mixture. Add the ricotta, blend again to combine fully, and season with salt and pepper to taste.

Also pictured: Gluten-Free Fennel Crackers (page 203)

Chapter 5

SKEWERS AND STICKS

BACK WHEN FONDUE WAS HAVING ITS MOMENT, my mom would pull out the hot pots, stands, skewers, and accompanying cans of Sterno and throw communal dipping parties. To my preteen eyes, this seemed both fancy and fun. So, during this era, when my birthday rolled around, fondue was my dinner of choice. Just as she'd done for guests, she'd set up two pots in the middle of the dining room table: one full of bubbling hot oil, the other full of molten cheese. Using the long silver skewers, we'd all spear shrimp and scallops to sizzle in the oil and stab at pieces of cauliflower, broccoli, and cherry tomatoes before dunking them into the melted cheese. It was, upon recollection, a kind of dinner theater, an interactive event, more about the entertainment factor than the food itself.

I've outgrown my desire for fondue, but the appeal of skewered ingredients is still, well, appealing to me. There's something playful about food on a stick. It's not the usual plate and fork scenario, so, like the fondue of bygone days, it's fun if not as affectedly fancy. And here's something else to keep in mind: Snacks served on skewers are a great way to branch out from cheese and charcuterie boards while still making the most of some of your favorite snacking ingredients.

Sure, boards have been the popular kids of the snacking world for some time now, the ones grabbing all the attention, but hear me out: Skewers are cool. Yes, boards are fashionable because they're about abundance, so many ingredients clustered together stylishly. And yes, skewers and sticks are a little more reserved, but they're edgy in their own right. They can still be about the cured meats and creamy cheeses, the sweetest fruits and freshest veg, but instead of bountiful, think thoughtful, poetic even. Instead of everything imaginable, imagine select things carefully curated and prettily combined.

The classic antipasti, when deconstructed and served as a skewer, starts and ends with a piece of rustic bread, all manner of cured meats and pickled vegetables sandwiched between them. Another stick might feature marinated feta mingling with cubes of watermelon and briny black olives for a summertime snack, while asparagus and gem lettuces can be grilled with lemons, then speared tightly together, with fresh burrata on the side. These are snacks with personality and depth, vibrant combinations that just cry out to be picked up and picked at.

Whether it's meatballs, set out with a few toothpicks, or melon ribbons threaded gracefully between tissue-thin slices of coppa, food that comes on or with a stick is fun and makes for easy snacking or whimsical entertaining. They may not yet be as trendy as boards (or fondue, for that matter), but I think their moment has arrived.

Antipasto Skewers

4 or 5 thick slices crusty bread, cut into 1-inch cubes

Extra-virgin olive oil

3 or 4 slices prosciutto, thinly sliced and torn in half

Marinated Baby Artichokes (page 76), or store-bought, drained and halved

6 small mozzarella cheese balls (bocconcini)

6 to 8 cherry tomatoes

6 slices soppressata, thinly sliced

3 or 4 slices of mortadella, halved

4 or 5 pepperoncini

6 to 8 marinated olives, pitted and drained

Fresh basil leaves

Red wine vinegar for serving (optional)

This little snack will win you friends, or make the ones you have love you even more. It's absurdly easy, can be mixed up in so many different ways that it never gets old, and it's what everyone loves in an antipasto or charcuterie and cheese board—variation—just sans the board. It also gives the cook (or, more accurately, the assembler) the opportunity to have fun curating lovely little selections that vary from stick to stick. The only guidelines I suggest in how you organize your skewers is to start and end with a hunk of (good quality) bread; it's a bit like a sandwich in that way, the bread punctuating delectable stuff in the middle. Otherwise, the key here is just to have fun: Combine finocchiona, coppa, or mortadella all on one skewer. Intersperse the charcuterie with different cheeses; think mozzarella, Asiago, provolone—or whatever you like best. And do not hesitate to mingle olives, pepperoncini, artichoke hearts, roasted peppers, or even caperberries together. The brinier, the better. **SERVES 4 TO 6**

Brush the bread with olive oil and lightly toast. Thread six skewers with a cube of bread followed by any combination or order of the following: a loosely folded piece of prosciutto, a halved artichoke heart, a mozzarella ball, a cherry tomato, a piece of soppressata, a slice of mortadella, a pepperoncini, an olive, and a basil leaf.

Place the skewers on a platter and drizzle lightly with olive oil and red wine vinegar, if desired, before serving.

Bresaola, Green Olives, and Parmesan

½ loaf of country-style bread (enough to get 12 chunks)

Extra virgin olive oil

Sea salt

Hunk of Parmesan (12 or more ounces)

24 Cerignola, Frescatrano, or other large green olives, pitted

12 slices bresaola

A beguiling claret-colored cured meat with delicate marbling, *bresaola* is similar in texture to prosciutto but is made from beef instead of pork and comes from the round cut of the steer, so it's very lean and tender with a deep, earthy flavor. I don't think it gets enough attention, certainly not the amount it deserves in light of how tasty it is. I first tried it in Rome, where it's often paired with arugula, Parmesan, and capers and gently doused in olive oil and lemon juice—the bitter greens, fatty cheese, and briny capers are the perfect counterbalance to the rich meat. This skewer mirrors that play of flavors—the rich with the tangy and buttery—but replaces the capers with succulent green olives. If you're looking to expand your charcuterie repertoire, I highly recommend bresaola as a starting place. **SERVES 6**

Preheat the broiler.

Cut or tear the bread into 12 large 2-inch chunks. Lightly brush or toss the bread with olive oil and sprinkle with a bit of salt and place on a baking sheet. Set the baking sheet under the broiler for a minute or two, turning the bread pieces once or twice so they toast lightly on all sides. Remove from the oven.

Use a knife to break off chunks of the Parmesan. You want these to be large enough to skewer but not as big as the pieces of toast. Don't worry if some of it crumbles—you can save the smaller pieces to serve alongside the sticks or to sprinkle on a salad later.

Thread a skewer with a chunk of the toasted bread, followed by a piece of the cheese, an olive, a folded slice of bresaola, and another olive. Repeat this process again so that each skewer has two pieces each of bread, cheese, and meat and four olives. Drizzle the skewers lightly with more olive oil and serve.

Seared Figs
with Stilton and Maple Pecans

1 cup pecans

3 tablespoons pure maple syrup

Pinch of sea salt

Pinch of ground cardamom

Pinch of cayenne pepper

12 figs, halved

12 ounces Stilton cheese

Someone will inevitably say I rely heavily on figs in my kitchen. They would not be wrong (I've heard the same about my use of anchovies, but it doesn't deter me). Figs are Mother Nature's candy. Here they're paired with sharp, creamy, slightly funky Stilton, and served with a smattering of sweetened nuts. This is the thing to serve in the fall, when the leaves crackle under foot and the air takes on the scent of woodsmoke. Pour yourself a glass of something red and warming and sit outside while you still can, enjoying the last of the violet hour with a fig. SERVES 6

Line a baking sheet with parchment paper and set aside.

In a large sauté pan, toast the pecans over medium heat, shaking the pan frequently to prevent them from burning, until they are very fragrant and just lightly coloring, 3 to 4 minutes. Add 2 tablespoons of the maple syrup—it will bubble up when it hits the hot pan so be careful—lower the heat to medium-low and toss the nuts to coat them evenly.

Add the salt and spices and continue cooking and stirring the nuts for another 3 minutes or so until the syrup has crystallized and is no longer shiny (you want the nuts to be candied, not just glazed). Transfer the pecans to the prepared baking sheet and let them cool completely.

Meanwhile, heat a small nonstick pan over medium-high heat. Brush the cut side of the figs lightly with the remaining 1 tablespoon of maple syrup and place the figs cut side down in the pan. Cook the figs until they are just beginning to brown on the edges, about 2 minutes (you don't want them to fall apart, just to warm through and caramelize a bit). Remove from the heat.

To serve, cut or break the Stilton into twelve small pieces, about 1 inch in diameter. Divide the seared figs and Stilton evenly among six skewers, alternating between the fruit and cheese. Serve the skewers on a platter with the maple pecans scattered on top.

Coppa with Melon Ribbons and Sheep's Cheese

1 medium cantaloupe

1 medium honeydew

6 ounces Ossau-Iraty, Pyrénées Brebis, or similar sheep's cheese

12 slices coppa

Extra-virgin olive oil for drizzling

Fresh tarragon leaves or fennel fronds for garnish

Flaky sea salt

Red pepper flakes

This simple skewer is a play on the classic cured meat and melon combo, but it replaces the prosciutto with the slightly less ubiquitous (but equally appetizing) coppa, which comes from the shoulder of the pig rather than the hind leg. And instead of simply wrapping chunks of melon in the cured meat, here you use a mandoline to make very thin, long ribbons of melon, strips that can be delicately threaded onto a skewer in a switchback pattern. Alternating the chiffon-like pieces of coppa with the fruit provides a familiar flavor combination, but in a uniquely appealing presentation. Interestingly, just by altering how you cut the melon and which kind of meat you use, this traditional concept takes on a very fresh feel (and taste). **SERVES 6**

Cut both melons in half and scoop out the seeds (save half of each melon for another use). Cut the melons into 2-inch pieces, then carefully cut off the rind. Use a mandoline to slice these pieces into long, thin ribbons.

Use a vegetable peeler to make thin slices of the cheese. You want at least two slices per skewer.

Skewer the melon ribbon by piercing each slice with the skewer at one end and then folding each ribbon back and forth, piercing with each fold, two or three times. Add a slice of the cheese, then fold a piece of the coppa in half and add this to the skewer. Repeat this pattern once more per skewer, adding an extra slice of melon at the end.

Drizzle the skewers lightly with olive oil, garnish with the fresh herbs, and sprinkle with the salt and red pepper flakes to taste.

Nectarines
with Prosciutto and Basil

12 slices prosciutto

2 to 3 nectarines, cut into ½-inch wedges

18 fresh basil leaves

Extra-virgin olive oil for drizzling

Flaky sea salt

Snacks do not need to be more than a few good things put together thoughtfully. They also don't need to be complicated, but it is nice when they surprise with a very minor tweak on tradition. While melon and prosciutto are inarguably a classic combination that need not be tinkered with for improvement, it's a combo that can be adjusted based on what you have in the house, what's in season, or simply what you feel like. Nectarines are one of my favorite stone fruits, because unlike the pure sweetness of peaches or the farinaceous texture of apricots, nectarines are slightly tangy and still juicy, an ideal complement to the salty earthiness of the prosciutto. They're not in season for that long, but when they're ripe, nectarines make a delightfully different pairing from the more expected melon; it's a subtle change but just enough of a surprise to be enticing. I serve these skewers with a glass of chilled Muscadet or Chablis and, if I'm feeling inspired, a lump of burrata or a soft cheese like Vermont Creamery's Coupole. SERVES 6

Cut or tear the prosciutto slices into thirds or quarters. Thread six skewers with a slice of nectarine followed by a loosely folded piece of prosciutto and a basil leaf. Repeat this pattern twice more per skewer so that each has at least three pieces of fruit, three pieces of prosciutto, and three basil leaves.

Place the skewers on a platter, drizzle lightly with olive oil, and sprinkle with a bit of salt before serving.

Grilled Chicken Satay
with Peanut-Coconut Sauce

4 boneless, skinless
chicken thighs, cut
into 1-inch pieces

1 teaspoon granulated
sugar

1 teaspoon sea salt

½ teaspoon freshly
ground black pepper

2 tablespoons toasted
sesame oil

One 1-inch piece
fresh ginger, peeled

1 garlic clove

½ cup creamy
unsweetened
peanut butter

¼ cup unsweetened
coconut milk, plus
more as needed

2 tablespoons soy sauce

1½ tablespoons freshly
squeezed lime juice,
plus wedges for serving

1 teaspoon light
brown sugar

¼ teaspoon red pepper
flakes, or to taste

Chicken thighs are underrated in my opinion. Not only are they very forgiving when it comes to cooking—they don't dry out as readily as breast meat does—they're also quite affordable. While darker than the breast, thigh meat isn't particularly gamey in flavor, so I find that even people who prefer white meat don't complain when served a nicely grilled thigh. In this preparation, the marinade relies on toasted sesame oil to lightly infuse the chicken with a hint of warmth and nuttiness. But the dipping sauce is really what it's all about—a simple puree designed to cosset the charred meat in peanut-y, coconut-y, creamy, tangy spiciness. I keep it on hand for more than just these satays, as the sauce is also brilliant dabbed on grilled shrimp or tofu, doused on noodles, or for simply dipping fresh veg when the mood strikes. SERVES 4 TO 6

In a medium bowl, combine the chicken with the granulated sugar, salt, black pepper, and sesame oil; toss to coat the chicken well. Cover and let the mixture marinate in the fridge for about 2 hours.

Meanwhile, in the bowl of a food processor, combine the ginger, garlic, peanut butter, coconut milk, soy sauce, lime juice, brown sugar, and red pepper flakes and puree until very smooth. Taste the sauce, adjust the seasoning, and add more coconut milk, if needed, to thin it a bit. Set the dipping sauce aside.

Preheat a gas grill to 400°F.

Thread the chicken pieces onto skewers (if you're using wooden skewers, soak them in water for about 10 minutes first), about three pieces per skewer. Cook the skewers for about 8 minutes total, turning at least once, until nicely browned and fully cooked through. Serve the chicken with the peanut dipping sauce and lime wedges.

Watermelon with Marinated Feta and Black Olives

1 lemon, cut into
6 slices

¾ cup extra-virgin
olive oil

1 teaspoon sugar

1 teaspoon fennel seeds

Juice of 1 lemon

One 8-ounce block
of good-quality feta
cheese, cut into
1-inch cubes

1 dried red chile

About 2 cups
2-inch-cubed
watermelon

12 or more black olives
(such as Kalamata,
Niçoise, or similar)

6 fresh mint leaves

Balsamic vinegar
for drizzling (optional)

This is all about the feta. Well, that's not fair, it's about the combination of sweet, juicy melon, the strong, fruity olives, *and* the roasted lemony feta, but it's the cheese that you're going to write home about. But here's the thing: You need good-quality feta cheese. What you want is a creamy, not-too-salty, not-too-dry feta, a block that tastes lovely on its own, because even though you're going to infuse it with other flavors, these are softer, subtle tastes that won't hide a strong, overly salty starting point. Lightly sugared, roasted lemons combined with the fennel seeds and a kick of red chile imparts a layered flavor to the feta—and that is what bounces off the watermelon and olives so brilliantly. I never hesitate to marinate the full block of feta either, even if I'm not serving a crowd, as any leftover marinated feta is gorgeous on a salad and it lasts in the fridge for a week or so. **SERVES 6**

Preheat the oven to 400°F. Place the lemon slices on a baking sheet and drizzle with about 2 tablespoons of the olive oil. Sprinkle the sugar and fennel seeds on top. Toss the lemons to coat well. Roast the slices until they just begin to color on the edges, 15 to 20 minutes. Remove the lemon slices from the oven and transfer to a medium bowl along with the remaining olive oil, the lemon juice, feta cubes, and chile. Cover and let the feta macerate for at least 2 hours or, preferably, overnight.

When you're ready to assemble the skewers, thread a cube of feta with a slice of the roasted lemon, a couple cubes of watermelon, an olive, and a mint leaf. Serve with a drizzle of balsamic vinegar, if desired.

Porchetta-Style Meatballs

3 tablespoons extra-virgin olive oil

1 medium shallot, finely diced

3 garlic cloves, grated

½ fennel bulb, trimmed, cored, and finely diced

2 teaspoons sea salt, plus more as needed

1 pound ground pork

2 slices thick-cut bacon (about 3 ounces), finely diced

1 large egg

1 cup bread crumbs, preferably homemade

½ cup grated Parmesan

¼ cup fennel fronds, roughly chopped

4 to 6 sprigs fresh rosemary, leaves removed and finely chopped

2 teaspoons fennel seeds

½ teaspoon red pepper flakes

Zest of 1 lemon

Freshly ground black pepper

The first real porchetta I tasted was at a weekday market in Umbria. There were multiple trucks all set up close to one another, somewhat separate from the cheese trucks and the vegetable stands, and each had a line, some longer than others, made up of locals who clearly had a favorite vendor. Jumping in one of the lines, not the longest but not the shortest either, we stood and watched men in white butcher coats slicing away at what looked to be highly varnished whole pigs, their skin like burnt amber. Not speaking Italian, we gathered from watching that you told the man in the truck how much pork you wanted by the number of people you were serving, and he carved his estimation of what that was off the pig. He then added a small piece of the crackling skin for each person and wrapped it all up in thick white paper. It's been years now, but I still remember the succulent and highly spiced meat—garlic, rosemary, an abundance of fennel—and the addictively crispy skin. It was a revelation. It was so Italian, so earthy and rustic and fatty and delicious. Sadly, there's no world where I'm going to roast a whole pig to snack on (every cook has their limits), but these meatballs are a fine approximation of the flavors that make porchetta so special. With an extra hit of fennel (I use the traditional fennel seeds but also add fresh fennel and fennel fronds), these take a fraction of the effort needed to roast a whole pig or fly to Italy. SERVES 6 TO 8

Preheat the oven to 400°F. Line a baking sheet with parchment paper and set aside.

In a medium frying pan, heat 2 tablespoons of the olive oil over medium heat until shimmering, about 1 minute. Add the diced shallot and cook, stirring frequently, 2 to 3 minutes, or until it just begins to soften. Add the garlic and cook until just fragrant, about 2 minutes. Add the diced fennel, season with a sprinkle of salt, and cook, stirring frequently for 6 to 7 minutes more, until the fennel and shallot are soft and translucent. Remove from the heat and transfer everything to a large bowl.

Add the pork, bacon, egg, bread crumbs, Parmesan, fennel fronds, rosemary, fennel seeds, red pepper flakes, lemon zest, 2 teaspoons salt, and a good grind of black pepper to the bowl with the cooked vegetables. Use your hands to mix the ingredients together thoroughly, being careful not to overhandle the mixture or it will become tough.

Panfry a test meatball to check the seasoning: Pull off about 2 tablespoons of the meat mixture and roll it between your hands to form a 1-inch-thick patty. In a small sauté pan, heat the remaining 1 tablespoon olive oil over medium-high until it shimmers. Fry the patty, about 2 minutes per side, or until fully cooked. When it's cool enough, taste for seasoning.

If you need to add any more salt, pepper, or anything to the mixture you can do it now; otherwise, pull off small fistfuls of the meat mixture, roll them into firm balls about 2 inches in diameter, and place them on the prepared baking sheet. Bake the meatballs, rotating the baking sheet once or twice, so the meatballs color on all sides, 18 to 20 minutes, or until cooked through.

Remove the pan from the oven and let the meatballs cool. Once they're cool enough to handle, arrange them on a platter with plenty of toothpicks nearby.

Grilled Asparagus and Little Gem Lettuce with Burrata

1 pound asparagus, trimmed and cut into 2-inch pieces

2 to 3 heads Little Gem (baby romaine) lettuce, quartered

2 lemons, thinly sliced

Extra-virgin olive oil for brushing and drizzling

Sea salt and freshly ground black pepper

One 4-ounce fresh ball burrata for serving

Charred toasts for serving (optional)

This recipe is an ode to spring. It's what I crave when I've eaten my weight in potatoes and hearty greens and am happy to banish winter for another year. When the first slim asparagus spears appear and the tender bundles of romaine are ready for picking, this is what you want to make. It's grilled, but only lightly, just enough to throw a green glow on the vegetables; the asparagus should still have a crispness in the center, and the gems should be charred but not totally wilted. And if you've never grilled gem lettuce before, it's like adding a newly discovered veg to your repertoire; be prepared to be delighted. Finished with a dish of creamy burrata, the only thing missing is some crusty bread and the sun on your skin. SERVES 4 TO 6

Preheat a gas grill to 400°F.

Brush the asparagus, lettuce, and lemon slices with enough olive oil to coat everything lightly. Fold three pieces of asparagus in a lemon slice and thread them together; repeat this on 8 to 12 skewers. (If you're using wooden skewers, soak them in water for about 10 minutes first.) Then add a quarter of a gem lettuce head to each skewer. (Each skewer should have one lemon-asparagus "cup" and one lettuce quarter.) Sprinkle the skewers with salt and pepper.

Transfer the skewers to the grill and cook, turning once, until the asparagus is bright green and just tender and the lettuce is charred and barely beginning to wilt, about 3 minutes.

Transfer the skewers to a platter and serve with a plate of the burrata, charred toasts (if using), and extra olive oil for drizzling.

Chapter 6

ONE PLATTER, MANY FORKS

WHEN IT COMES TO SHARING FOOD, THERE ARE TWO KINDS OF PEOPLE: Those who love to reach across the table for a taste without a second thought and those who will take your hand off with a butter knife if you so much as glance at their plate. I fall very solidly into the "what's mine is ours and what's yours is too" category. Even before the small plate thing was a real thing, the idea of ordering food at a restaurant and not being able to tuck into more than mine was anathema. But, then, I grew up in a family that intentionally ordered different things precisely so we could all taste one another's. It didn't occur to me until later in life that there were people who didn't think sharing was the entire idea behind going out to eat.

But things changed with the pandemic. Suddenly the world was suffering from an illness that demanded we distance ourselves to save ourselves. We masked and disinfected with fear for our health at the forefront of our minds, and the idea of sharing anything with anyone outside what we were now calling our "pods" was truly scary. As those first winter days, when we were cocooned in our respective homes, turned into summer months, seeing a few friends outside became acceptable again, granted you kept your distance and didn't mingle the glasses or the silverware.

During this time Ken and I took to setting up separate little duos on the patio, each with two chairs, a small table, two glasses and a bottle each of water and wine. For these intimate adventures (for that's what they felt like in the midst of so much solitude), I made small grazing boards, each one a miniature version of something I would have done more grandly in previous days. No one had to wonder or worry, as each couple had their own little bubble of food and beverages. It was strange and stilted at first (remembering not to hug each other, jumping back when you realized you'd stepped a bit too close), but we were together and sharing some semblance of what used to be normal.

How far we've come. For a time, it seemed as though the world had spun off its axis, everything was so unsteady, it was fair to wonder if we'd ever be able to touch each other again without hesitating, without thinking twice. Now it's almost hard to believe we were ever that frightened. It's also hard to fathom the fear we had of sharing food. But it was there and it's taken some rejiggering to let go of all that concern.

I think many of us are changed since the pandemic. I certainly am, and my compromise, my internal rules for dealing with this new normal, are these: Mask when needed, hug as freely as you can, and make lots of platters intended for sharing. Big platters full of flavor jumbled together and meant for many forks mingling at once. Pretty platters loaded with ingredients that are too delicious to resist. What I want now is to, along with a few friends, dig straight into a salad and not feel the need for plates or the necessity to serve it more formally. What I love is to scoop up a slice of socca or a sliver of a tlayuda from one shared dish without pause and know that those sharing the table feel just as free. I know this could change again, and I don't take the pleasure of communal eating for granted.

That's what this chapter is all about. It's for those of us with the instinct to eat off one another's plate built into our DNA—you know who you are—and for you the idea of one platter and many forks will be enchanting, if not already familiar. For those of you who still find sharing food unappealing, don't turn away. You're totally invited. Just bring your own plate.

Stone Fruit Salad with Tomatoes and Mozzarella

2 peaches or nectarines, pitted and cut into ½-inch pieces

2 cups cherry tomatoes (yellow and red), halved

½ small red onion, thinly sliced into half-moons

3 ounces fresh mozzarella, torn into bite-size pieces

2 to 3 tablespoons extra-virgin olive oil

Juice of 1 lemon

2 cups halved, pitted cherries

3 or 4 stems basil, leaves picked

Flaky sea salt

There's a salad stuck in my memory from a work trip to New Zealand that I've never been able to replicate perfectly. It was a cherry salad, a sizable plate filled with almost nothing but the deep crimson fruit, all nestled together and draped in a frisky shallot vinaigrette, then dotted with tangy bits of goat cheese. It was bewitching not just because it was a salad made from almost entirely cherries (how simple, how clever) but also because the dressing was so blatantly savory, so when paired with summer's sweetest fruits the contrast was stark, bracing, and utterly seductive. The notion of a cherry-only salad was so novel to me that, as I was eating it, I repeatedly felt as though I was being tricked: Were these actually cherries or just wildly sweet tomatoes? Who had come up with this idea, and why wasn't it me? All this is a prelude to admitting that I stole the cherry idea. I purloined the concept and added it shamelessly to a salad that I have been making for years during summer's peak, when peaches are blushing their deepest shades, when tomatoes abound in every conceivable color, and when the smell of basil overtakes you when you accidentally brush by it in the garden. Add the cherries to this union (no need for the shallot, the red onion is there doing the same job) and some creamy mozzarella, and now you have something arguably less brilliant but, for my money, more complete—so much of what I love about summer together in one dish. SERVES 4 TO 6

In a large bowl, combine the peaches, tomatoes, onion, and mozzarella. Drizzle everything lightly with the olive oil and lemon juice. Toss the mixture to combine, then add the cherries, and toss again very gently (if you're too aggressive here the entire salad will turn purple with cherry juice, and you want the different colors to show as well as the vibrant flavors).

Transfer the salad to a large platter and add a generous amount of basil. Sprinkle with salt and serve.

Fig Panzanella
with Prosciutto and Goat Cheese

½ loaf day-old rustic
bread

½ cup extra-virgin olive
oil, plus more as needed

2 tablespoons freshly
squeezed lemon juice

2 tablespoons red wine
vinegar

1 teaspoon honey

Sea salt and freshly
ground black pepper

1 small head radicchio

10 to 12 fresh figs,
quartered

½ small red onion,
very thinly sliced
into half-moons

2 handfuls of baby
arugula

6 to 8 slices prosciutto

4 ounces goat cheese

Fresh basil leaves
for garnish

The traditional Italian bread salad, panzanella, is gorgeous when
made traditionally: crusty bread, tomatoes, capers, olives, hearts of
celery if you like, all sopping up a delectable vinaigrette. But take the
main idea, the irresistible day-old bread soaked in tangy goodness,
and have some fun. Add syrup-sweet figs, smoky prosciutto, bitter
radicchio ribbons, peppery arugula leaves, and some tart goat
cheese just at the end. Admittedly a vast departure from the classic,
an interpretation that veers away from the expected, but one that
echoes the original with deeply vibrant flavors. It's quite a looker too.
SERVES 4 TO 6

Make sure your bread is truly stale—if not, cut the bread into thick
slices and then tear the bread into big pieces (about 1 inch) and let it
sit out in the air for an hour or more or toast it for a couple of minutes,
not for color but just to dry it out. You want about 4 cups of bread.

In a small bowl or jar, combine the olive oil, lemon juice, vinegar,
and honey with some salt and pepper; whisk or shake well. Taste the
dressing and adjust the seasoning as needed.

In a large bowl, drizzle the bread with half the dressing, tossing
to coat. Cut the radicchio into ribbons and add it to the bowl along
with the figs and onion, then toss to combine and let it all sit for a few
minutes so the flavors meld. Meanwhile, tear each slice of prosciutto
into four or so pieces.

Add the arugula to the bowl, along with the prosciutto, and
drizzle with more of the dressing. Toss again. Transfer the salad to
a large platter and dot it with pieces of the goat cheese and the basil
to serve.

Also pictured: Carta di Musica (page 192)

Also pictured: Spanish-Style BLT (page 67)

Tortilla with Jamón and Shrimp

6 medium shrimp, shelled, tails removed, and deveined

½ cup extra-virgin olive oil, plus more as needed

Sea salt and freshly ground black pepper

¼ teaspoon pimentón (Spanish smoked paprika)

1 large sweet onion (such as Vidalia), thinly sliced into half-moons

4 medium russet potatoes, peeled

5 large eggs

2 or 3 slices jamón, cut into small dice

My first experience with an authentic Spanish tortilla was in Seville many moons ago. Ken and I took a trip to the south of Spain and spent the entire two weeks eating our way around Andalusia, with necessary breaks in consumption to take in the remarkable architecture and breathtaking countryside. Call me a philistine, but for me it was really about the food. I could wax on about the garlic shrimp bubbling in olive oil served tableside, the meaty Sevillano olives, the earthy Ibérico ham made from acorn-fed pigs, the bocadillo—small sandwiches on crusty baguette . . . but what is still most dreamy to me about that trip is the tortilla. Layers of tender potatoes nestled in onions and eggs and cooked gently, until the onions almost melt and the potatoes are just toothsome enough that you feel the collapse of each layer as you bite. What I've done with my version here is to add some of the stunning, smoky flavor of pimentón-spiked shrimp and a bit of nutty jamón into the mix, so it's more than just that sublime tangle of eggs, onions, and potatoes—but a collection of many Spanish flavors all in one. PS: The soaking of the par-cooked potatoes in the egg mixture is essential—please don't skip this step or you will be disappointed. SERVES 6 TO 8

Using a very sharp knife, slice the shrimp lengthwise, cutting all the way through so that you have two flat halves. Then cut each half again crosswise into four small pieces.

In a 10-inch nonstick skillet, heat 1 tablespoon of the olive oil over medium heat, then add the shrimp pieces. Sprinkle the shrimp with a bit of salt and pepper and the pimentón, toss to coat well, and cook until just pink, about 2 minutes—they'll continue to cook when added to the potato mixture. Remove the shrimp from the pan and set aside; reserve the pan.

In a separate large sauté pan, heat 3 tablespoons of the olive oil over medium-high heat. When the oil shimmers, add the onion and sprinkle with salt and pepper. Lower the heat to medium-low, adding a bit more olive oil if the pan seems dry, and continue cooking until the onion begins to soften but isn't browning, 8 to 10 minutes.

(recipe continues)

Meanwhile, use a mandoline to slice the potatoes. You want them to be very thin, about ⅛ inch. When the onions are tender and golden, add the potatoes and continue cooking over medium-low heat, tossing frequently (try not to break up the potatoes if you can avoid it). The pan will seem very full, but that's okay; continue tossing the potatoes every couple of minutes and separating them from one another so they all partially cook, 8 to 12 minutes.

Meanwhile, beat the eggs in a bowl large enough to hold the potato-onion mixture and season with salt and pepper. Remove the potato-onion mixture from the heat and let it cool slightly (if you add it directly to the eggs, you'll cook them). When cool, add the onion-potato mixture to the eggs along with the reserved shrimp and the chopped jamón. Stir to combine, then let it sit for about 15 minutes so the potatoes absorb some of the eggs and the flavors meld.

In the nonstick pan you used to cook the shrimp, heat the remaining ¼ cup olive oil over medium-high heat. Add the egg-potato mixture and, using a silicone spatula, gently spread it out evenly, making sure the potatoes are tucked in at the edges and layered relative neatly and that the egg is evenly distributed. Cook for about 1 minute (the oil should be bubbling at the edges) to develop a nice crust, then lower the heat to low and cook until the underside and edges of the tortilla are set, about 15 minutes.

While the tortilla continues to cook, preheat the broiler.

When the tortilla is set on the edges but still loose in the middle, carefully transfer it to the oven. Watching closely, broil for 1 to 2 minutes, just long enough to set the top. Remove the tortilla from the broiler and shake the pan to loosen it, using a spatula if necessary.

Place a plate the same size as the pan on top of the tortilla, flip it, and slide it back into the pan, cooked side up. Continue cooking the tortilla over low heat until it's fully set and moves around easily in the pan, another 7 to 8 minutes. Invert the tortilla again once it's finished cooking. Serve hot or at room temperature.

Mediterranean Farro Salad with Olives and Parsley

1 cup farro

¼ cup extra-virgin olive oil

Juice of 1 lemon

Sea salt and freshly ground black pepper

1 Persian cucumber, cut into ¼-inch pieces

½ small red onion, finely chopped

½ cup chopped pitted Kalamata olives

About 12 cherry tomatoes, quartered

½ cup canned chickpeas, rinsed and drained

Handful of flat-leaf parsley (15 to 18 stems), leaves picked and finely chopped

Splash of red wine vinegar (optional)

To my mind farro is the perfect grain: It's nutty, earthy, a bit chewy, and works just as well when prepared like risotto for a warming winter meal as it does the base of a salad like this one. Think of this as an unconventional take on tabouleh: lots of verdant parsley, briny olives, and creamy chickpeas topped off with a tangy lemon dressing. It works brilliantly as a summer snack on the patio or an easy make-ahead platter during the cooler months when you crave something resonant of sunnier days. This is also ideal travel fare; in fact, this is my go-to airplane snack because it only gets better as it macerates in the dressing and is best served at room temperature. If you ever sit next to me on a plane, you'll know. I'll be the one with the Tupperware of this salad on my tray table and the tang of lemon vinaigrette wafting nearby. SERVES 4 TO 6

Cook the farro according to package directions. While still warm, transfer the farro to a large bowl. Drizzle with the olive oil, add the lemon juice, and season with salt and pepper. Add the cucumber, onion, olives, tomatoes, chickpeas, and parsley to the bowl and toss to combine well. Add the red wine vinegar (if using) and mix again. Adjust the seasonings as needed. You can serve immediately, but if you have the time, let the salad rest at room temperature for about 30 minutes so the flavors meld.

Spiced Lamb Flatbreads with Lemony Hummus

¼ to ½ cup extra-virgin olive oil

1 small red onion, finely diced

2 garlic cloves, grated

1 pound ground lamb

2 teaspoons ground cumin, plus more as needed

Sea salt and freshly ground black pepper

One 14-ounce can chickpeas, rinsed and drained (or 2 cups cooked)

2 tablespoons freshly squeezed lemon juice, plus more as needed

6 pieces Middle Eastern–Style Flatbread (page 195)

Shredded lettuce

2 to 3 large ripe tomatoes, chopped

1 English cucumber or 3 Persian cucumbers, chopped

2 avocados, halved, pitted, and diced

1 cup pitted Kalamata olives

2 sprigs mint leaves, picked and chopped

We have been making these for years and call them Greek tostadas because they are reminiscent of the tostadas I grew up eating in LA as a kid (crispy tortillas layered with beans, ground meat, lettuce, salsa, and guacamole) but with Mediterranean flavors instead of Mexican. These aren't fancy, they shouldn't be fussy, and they will probably get a bit messy as it is just a tumble of delicious food mounded on top of a piece of bread. Feel free to add marinated artichokes or pepperoncini if you want, play with the amounts of everything as suits your mood, but do make your own hummus. You can buy decent flatbreads these days, so don't feel like you have to make your own, but if you have the time and inclination, why not? Try the Middle Eastern–Style Flatbread on page 195. **SERVES 4 TO 6**

Preheat the oven to 300°F.

In a medium frying pan, heat 1 tablespoon of the olive oil over medium heat until shimmering, about 1 minute. Add the onion and cook, stirring frequently until it just begins to soften, about 3 minutes. Add half the grated garlic and cook until fragrant, another 2 minutes. Add the ground lamb, season with 1 teaspoon of the cumin, a bit of salt and some pepper, and cook, stirring frequently, until the lamb is cooked through and no longer pink, 6 to 7 minutes. Remove the pan from the heat and set aside.

Meanwhile, in the bowl of a food processor, blitz the chickpeas and the remaining garlic until the mixture is coarsely chopped. With the machine running, stream in ¼ cup of the olive oil. Continue to process until the mixture is smooth, adding more oil until you have a creamy puree.

Add the lemon juice, the remaining 1 teaspoon cumin, and salt and pepper and pulse. Taste and adjust the flavor as needed.

When you're ready to serve, put the flatbreads on a baking sheet, brush them with olive oil, and sprinkle with a little bit of sea salt. Place in the oven to gently warm, about 5 minutes.

To serve, spread a generous ¼ cup or so of the hummus on each flatbread, add a scoop of the lamb to each, and top with the lettuce, tomatoes, cucumber, avocado, and olives. Garnish with mint.

Communal Shrimp and Crab Cocktail via Baja

¼ cup Old Bay

1 small white onion, quartered

2 pounds large unpeeled shrimp

1 cup ketchup

About 6 tablespoons freshly squeezed lime juice (from 3 to 4 limes), plus more for serving

2 tablespoons tequila

½ teaspoon Tabasco, or similar hot sauce, or to taste

Pinch of cayenne, or to taste

Sea salt and freshly ground black pepper

1 pound cooked fresh lump crabmeat

3 or 4 stems cilantro, leaves picked and chopped

3 avocados, halved and pitted

Tortilla chips for serving

Sometimes you just want to feel like you're sitting by the sea, your hair going a bit wild in the salty air, and your shoulders soaking up the sun. And if you actually are, well, all the better. But if you aren't, here's the thing to do: Get some fresh shrimp and crab, a few avocados, and a bag of good chips. In just a few minutes (as long as it takes to boil the shrimp and mix a quick tequila-laced cocktail sauce), you'll be mentally transported south of the border. No, you don't need to bother peeling or deveining the shrimp, but yes, you do want to use a really generous amount of Old Bay in the boil. I serve the lightly seasoned crab in the avocado halves, but I often find I have more crab than avocados. I remedy this excess by putting the rest of the crab in a small bowl on the side for scooping with the chips. Serve this with Rhubarb Margaritas (page 242) for the full effect. SERVES 6

Fill the bottom of a large bowl with ice. Bring a large pot of salted water to a boil and add the Old Bay and the onion. Working in batches so as not to overcrowd the pot, add the shrimp and poach them until pink and opaque, about 2 minutes. Use a slotted spoon to remove the shrimp from the water and transfer them to the bowl of ice. When all the shrimp are cooked, put the bowl in the fridge.

While the shrimp chill, make the cocktail sauce by combining the ketchup, 2 tablespoons of the lime juice, the tequila, and the hot sauce. Season the mix with cayenne, salt, and black pepper, adjusting the flavors as you see fit.

In a small bowl, season the crab with 2 tablespoons of the lime juice and salt and black pepper. Add the cilantro and toss well; taste and add more lime juice or salt and pepper if needed. Season the top of each avocado half with a bit of salt and black pepper and the remaining lime juice (this will also help them from browning) and then spoon the crab mixture into the avocado halves. Serve the shrimp on a tray surrounding the cocktail sauce and alongside the crab-filled avocado halves and tortilla chips.

Also pictured: Rhubarb Margarita (page 242)

Italian Tuna Salad with Potato Chips

1 small shallot, finely chopped

⅓ cup extra-virgin olive oil

Juice of 1 lemon, plus more as needed

Splash of red wine vinegar or sherry vinegar, plus more as needed

1 teaspoon Dijon mustard

1 teaspoon whole-grain Dijon mustard

Sea salt and freshly ground black pepper

7 to 8 ounces baby arugula

1 Persian cucumber, or ½ English cucumber, sliced

1 cup canned cannellini beans or chickpeas, rinsed and drained

1 small fennel bulb, trimmed and quartered

One 6- to 8-ounce jar Italian tuna fillets in olive oil

2 avocados, halved and pitted

2 cups Cape Cod potato chips, gently crushed

This salad started as a very solitary affair. Whenever I found myself alone in the house wanting a substantial snack, but not necessarily feeling the urge to cook, this salad became my table-for-one treat. Soon I was making this when my friend Kate came around, and then Andie and Mal were introduced and joined the coven as well. Now this salad is a communal platter tossed together so frequently it's almost embarrassing. The only new addition is the potato chips and here's why: Cape Cod potato chips are my weakness, and I regularly grab a handful (okay, two) and eat them with the salad. But recently I realized it's even better when they're crushed up and tossed in—they alleviate the need for croutons, replace bread, and generally make it irresistible. As for the dressing, I'm partial to mixing my mustards, as the Dijon emulsifies while the whole grain adds texture, but if you have only one in the house, don't fret—either will work fine. Whatever you do, don't skip the chips. SERVES 4

In a lidded jar (10 to 12 ounces), combine the shallot, olive oil, lemon juice, vinegar, and mustards. Shake the jar vigorously to emulsify the dressing. Taste, then season with salt and pepper. Adjust the flavors as needed with more lemon juice, vinegar, or salt and pepper. Set aside.

Put the arugula in a large salad bowl and add the cucumber and beans. Adjust a mandoline to a very fine setting, then carefully shave the fennel into the bowl—you want the fennel to be paper-thin. Drain the tuna and add it to the bowl, using a fork to break it up.

Cut the avocados into thin slices lengthwise and set them aside while you dress the salad with the vinaigrette. Toss well. Add 1 cup of the potato chips to the bowl just before serving and toss again. To serve, transfer the salad to a large platter and add the sliced avocado and remaining cup of chips on top. Serve any leftover dressing on the side.

Kasha, Pasta, and Vegetable Frittata

2 tablespoons extra-virgin olive oil

¼ small red onion, cut into thin half-moons

6 to 8 cremini or similar mushrooms, quartered

Sea salt and freshly ground black pepper

8 cherry tomatoes, quartered

4 large eggs

¼ cup Parmesan, finely grated

½ cup cooked kasha

About 1 cup cooked cut pasta

1 cup baby spinach or arugula

Once upon a time I made a pot of kasha varnishkes (a traditionally Jewish recipe that combines caramelized onions, bowtie pasta, and toasted kasha, aka buckwheat), and we had leftovers. Ken took it upon himself to look up something new to do with leftover pasta and stumbled on a noodle frittata recipe in a cookbook by Patricia Wells—basically scrambled eggs with pasta. Figuring a bit of kasha couldn't hurt, he took whatever veg we had and tossed it with the varnishkes and some eggs. This is the happy outcome of that mingling of ideas. The kasha becomes akin to sausage crumbles (a wildly nice thing when your vegetarian pals come around), and the pasta gets a bit crispy thanks to the second turn in the pan. SERVES 4 TO 6

Preheat the broiler.

In a medium nonstick skillet, heat the olive oil over medium heat. When the oil is hot, add the onion, lower the heat to medium-low, and cook, stirring occasionally, until it begins to soften, 2 to 3 minutes.

Add the mushrooms, season with salt and pepper, and cook until they release their juices and the liquid evaporates, 6 to 8 minutes. Add the tomatoes and cook until the skins soften and the juices release, another 3 minutes.

Meanwhile, in a small bowl, beat the eggs until fully blended. Stir in the Parmesan and a sprinkle of salt and pepper.

Add the cooked pasta to the pan with the mushrooms, stir, and let the pasta absorb the flavor, about 2 minutes. Stir in the kasha and cook for 2 to 3 minutes. At this point, the tomato juices should have evaporated and everything should be glistening.

Add the eggs, making sure to distribute them evenly, and turn the heat to low. Cook for about 5 minutes, then use a silicone spatula to gently release the edges. When the eggs are mostly set but slightly loose in the middle, add the greens and let them wilt for about 1 minute.

Transfer the pan to the broiler and cook until the edges are puffed and beginning to color, about 2 minutes. Serve immediately or at room temperature.

Also pictured: Creamy Tomatillo Salsa (page 133) and Charred Corn and Nectarine Relish (page 131)

Oaxacan-Style Tlayudas with Mushroom-Quinoa "Chorizo"

2 cups water

1 cup red quinoa, rinsed

3 tablespoons extra-virgin olive oil

½ sweet onion (such as Vidalia), finely chopped

1 garlic clove, grated

16 ounces cremini mushrooms, roughly chopped

2 tablespoons chili powder

1 tablespoon ground cumin

1 tablespoon pimentón (Spanish smoked paprika)

1 teaspoon oregano

1 teaspoon garlic powder

Pinch of cayenne pepper, or to taste

1 teaspoon sea salt, or to taste

1 teaspoon freshly ground black pepper

1 tablespoon tomato paste

4 to 6 large flour tortillas (I usually use 14-inch tortillas)

A standard of Oaxacan fare, tlayudas are very large crispy fried tortillas that are smeared with beans, then topped with lettuce or cabbage, salsa, cheese, and sometimes meat—my idea of the ultimate shared plate. The ones I've had are always quite big, about the size of a large pizza, so the slender slices are perfect for grazing with a group. What makes this version different from any that I've had before is that instead of meat, this relies on vegan "chorizo," made from a combination of red quinoa and mushrooms. The quinoa provides a texture similar to ground sausage, and the mushrooms offer up a meatiness that, when combined, makes for a rich, spicy, crumbled blend (when you're cooking for a bigger group, this vegan-and-vegetarian-friendly blend meets a lot of dietary desires). Obviously, you can use this chorizo in other preparations, but I find it perfect here as omnivores are loath to miss the meat and the more finicky eaters are thrilled to have something made with them in mind. Add to this a generous smear of Black Bean Spread (page 130), a liberal drizzle of Creamy Tomatillo Salsa (page 133), and a lavish topping of Charred Corn and Nectarine Relish (page 131) and you can do something quite hard with ease—make everyone happy. **SERVES 6 TO 8 WITH LEFTOVERS TO FREEZE**

To make the "chorizo," bring the water to a boil in a medium saucepan. Add the quinoa and 1 tablespoon of the olive oil, lower the heat to a simmer, then cook for 15 to 20 minutes. You'll know the quinoa is ready when the grain has popped open and you see the germ of the kernel; at this point, if the water has not all been absorbed, drain the quinoa and set aside.

In a large saucepan, heat the remaining 2 tablespoons olive oil over medium heat until shimmering, about 1 minute. Add the chopped onion and cook, stirring frequently until it just begins to soften, 5 to 6 minutes. Add the grated garlic and cook until just fragrant, another minute or two. Add the chopped mushrooms and cook, stirring occasionally, until their liquid releases and evaporates, another 6 to 8 minutes.

(recipe and ingredients continue)

Vegetable or other
neutral oil for frying

2 cups Black Bean
Spread with Pickled
Radishes (page 130)

About 1 cup grated
white Cheddar or Jack
cheese, or crumbled
queso fresco

Charred Corn and
Nectarine Relish
(page 131)

Creamy Tomatillo Salsa
(page 133)

Meanwhile, in a small bowl, combine the chili powder, cumin, pimentón, oregano, garlic powder, cayenne, salt, and black pepper. Set aside.

When the mushrooms are very tender, the pan is mostly dry, and they are just beginning to caramelize on the edges, add the cooked quinoa to the pan and lower the heat to low. Stir in the tomato paste, then add the spice mixture and mix well to combine. Cook for another 3 to 4 minutes to give the flavors a chance to meld a bit and warm through. Remove the mixture from the heat and set aside. The blend can also be frozen in airtight containers at this point and will last for up to 3 months.

Preheat the broiler. Line a baking sheet or cooling rack with paper towels.

In a pan large enough to fit a single tortilla, heat ¼ cup oil over medium-high heat. When the oil shimmers, add a tortilla to the pan. Lower the heat to medium-low and rotate the tortilla continuously so it crisps without overcooking. When the tortilla has bubbled in places and is golden brown, remove it to drain on the prepared baking sheet and continue with another tortilla. When you have enough tortillas to accommodate your guests (depending on how large the tortillas are, you may need more or less), you can begin to build the tlayudas.

Lay the fried tortillas on baking sheets and spread the black beans evenly around the center of the fried tortillas as you would tomato sauce on a pizza (reserve the pickled radishes from that recipe for serving). Top the sauce with a handful of cheese and transfer the tortillas to the oven to quickly melt the cheese; watch them carefully as you don't want the edges to burn. Remove the tortillas from the oven and layer the cheese with a generous amount of the "chorizo" (about 1 cup per tortilla depending on how large they are). To serve, top each tortilla with a bit of the corn relish, a drizzle of tomatillo salsa, and some of the reserved pickled radishes. Slice into pieces and serve with more of everything on the side.

Miso Caesar with Asparagus, Peas, and Prosciutto Crumble

¾ cup extra-virgin olive oil

2 to 3 slices prosciutto

2 garlic cloves, smashed, plus 1 garlic clove, grated

2 cups bread crumbs, preferably homemade

¼ teaspoon red pepper flakes, or to taste

Sea salt and freshly ground black pepper

3 to 4 anchovy fillets

Juice of 2 lemons

1 teaspoon white miso

1 bunch of asparagus, trimmed

1 cup fresh peas

6 to 8 heads Little Gem (baby romaine) lettuce, or 3 to 4 romaine hearts, leaves separated

Freshly shaved Parmesan for topping

Focaccia Crisps (page 187; optional)

A good Caesar salad is sort of a unicorn. For as often as they're on a menu, I find them to be dependably disappointing if not inedible. The romaine is frequently tough or wilted, the croutons are likely out of a box or at least flavorless and stale, the cheese, if there at all, is often grated (a true misstep in my opinion), and the dressing is reliably dreadful. Certainly, there are the ones that delight, but in my experience, they are few and far between. This Caesar aims to make up for what so many of the sad ones lack: It stays true to tradition (good ingredients treated well) but also strays just enough to make it special. Miso added to the dressing gives it a bit of an umami boost, while asparagus and peas provide some textural contrast to the baby romaine. All that and, instead of croutons, homemade bread crumbs with toasted prosciutto shards to give you a bit of salty crunch in every bite. (One of my regular salad tricks is to use bread crumbs in lieu of croutons, as they integrate more fully, so instead of a big bite of crispiness every now and then, you're rewarded with constant crunch.) Finished with large shavings of fresh Parmesan, this is the kind of Caesar salad I dream of. But if after tasting it you remain unconverted to bread crumbs over croutons, Focaccia Crisps (page 187) served on the side should placate you. **SERVE 4 TO 6**

Preheat the oven to 375°F. Line a baking sheet with parchment paper.

Lay the prosciutto on the prepared baking sheet. Transfer the baking sheet to the oven and cook until the prosciutto begins to crisp and curl on the edges, about 10 minutes. Remove from the oven and set aside to cool.

Meanwhile, in a large skillet, heat ¼ cup of the olive oil over medium heat. Add the smashed garlic and cook until just fragrant, about 1 minute. Add the bread crumbs and red pepper flakes and season with salt and black pepper. Lower the heat to medium-low and continue to cook, stirring frequently to keep the crumbs from burning, until they're golden brown, about 10 minutes. Remove from the heat, pull out and discard the garlic, and let the bread crumbs cool to crisp up.

(recipe continues)

When the prosciutto is cool enough to handle (it should be very crunchy), break it into small pieces and add it to the toasted bread crumbs.

To make the dressing, use a chef's knife to finely chop the anchovies. Then, using the flat side of the knife, mash them a bit. Add the remaining grated garlic and continue, using the flat side of the knife, to spread the anchovy-garlic mixture back and forth until you have a relatively smooth paste. Put the paste in a lidded jar (10 to 12 ounces) and add the remaining ½ cup olive oil, the lemon juice, miso, and a generous amount of black pepper. Stir the dressing to incorporate the miso and then shake it vigorously to emulsify the dressing. Taste and adjust the seasoning as needed. Set aside (if you have the foresight, make the dressing a day in advance to help the flavors meld).

Bring a medium pot of salted water to a boil over high heat. Add the asparagus and peas and cook until the water returns to a boil and the vegetables are bright green, about 2 minutes. Drain immediately into a colander and run the vegetables under cold water to stop the cooking process. When the asparagus spears are cool to the touch, cut them into bite-size pieces.

To assemble the salad, put the lettuce leaves in a large bowl along with the asparagus and peas. Dress the salad and toss to coat everything well. Transfer the salad to a large platter and top with lots of Parmesan shavings and the prosciutto crumble. Serve with the focaccia crisps alongside, if desired.

Also pictured: Focaccia Crisps (page 187)

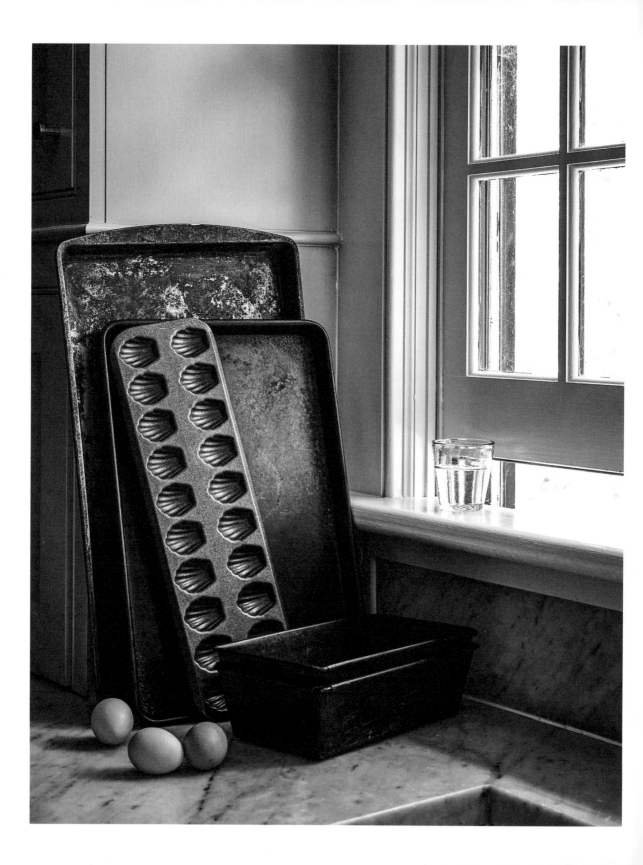

Chapter 7

BAKING SHEETS AND BREAD BASKETS

I FALL IN LOVE, OR AT LEAST FIND MYSELF DEEPLY INFATUATED, quite easily. Especially when it comes to breads and crunchy snacks that beguile me with their golden color and winsome salted crusts. I spy them at the markets in their peek-a-boo plastic bags and artisanal-style boxes and my heart leaps: At last, I've found my new favorite carb-y thing. But often, just as quickly as I go weak in the knees for these seductive snacks, my heart breaks just a little when I try them and find them wanting—lacking that crunch, that chew, that special something.

Yes, almost every time I buy a box of breadsticks or a bag of taralli, I am disappointed in the flavor, let down by their freshness, and generally sad that they aren't better. They should be. Why is it so hard to make a great cracker or a mind-blowing focaccia? It isn't. Which is why I choose, most of the time, to make my own, and I'm hoping you might as well.

Certainly with the advent of more artisanal producers, these basics have improved a lot in recent years. But along with that upgrade has also come an uptick in prices. Spending upward of six dollars for a box of crackers for cheese or sticks for snacking seems silly to me if I can make them better myself for a fraction of the price. I'll allow that this takes some time and effort, and admittedly, the recipes in this chapter are more time intensive and labor laden than most of the others in this book. Some rely on yeast and the time it takes for dough to rise, some need to be rolled flat or twisted round, and all need a little more attention to detail than opening a box or slicing a store-bought loaf. But they are worth it, I promise. A baking sheet of focaccia (ten minutes to mix the dough, two days fully unattended in the fridge) is a declaration of love to anyone you share it with. A jar of breadsticks, a dish of tarallini, or a tumble of madeleines, these all require some sweat equity, but the accolades and affection you'll reap from those who enjoy them will leave you glowing.

Cooking for others is a gift, and there are certain foods that elevate that offering to the more spectacular, the more monumental. Breads and crackers, those things that we so commonly buy because it's so much easier—those are the things that earn real bragging rights when made by hand. They surprise and delight because they are a blatantly unnecessary but absolutely lovely thing to do. "You *made* these?" is the exclamation of disbelief that I bet you'll hear when you set out a plate of brittle Carta di Musica (page 192) or a tower of Middle Eastern–Style Flatbreads (page 195), followed quickly by "You're amazing."

Focaccia with Caramelized Onions and Thyme

1 teaspoon active dry yeast

¼ teaspoon sugar

3½ cups warm water (about 110°F or roughly the feel of your skin's temperature)

7 cups (980 grams) all-purpose flour

2 tablespoons kosher salt

8 tablespoons olive oil, plus more for fingers

1 large Vidalia or other sweet onion, thinly sliced

Sea salt

Fresh thyme leaves, to taste

Flaky sea salt

I learned how to make this focaccia from a chef in Ghent, New York. A fantastic cook and lovely human, I met Mimi when I was invited to teach food styling at a photography workshop being held at the farm she owned with her husband, Richard. The night prior to the workshop, Mimi always prepared a family-style dinner for the group, and this was reason enough for me to make the annual trip. She'd roast one of their farm-raised Berkshire pigs, serve a stunning array of just-picked baby root vegetables and grilled heads of Little Gem lettuce drizzled with nothing more than lemon juice, and then present a locally sourced cheese plate along with squares of this fabulous focaccia topped with piney rosemary and flaky salt. The meal was only further enhanced by the view: acres of grassy open land and rolling hills, the air humming with insects and vibrating with evening birdsong—the way it does when spring is just starting to fade and summer is on the edge of wandering in.

All of it was lovely, but as an avid bread baker, this focaccia captivated me. Never sure how a cook will respond to a request for a recipe, I was hesitant, but Mimi generously did what the best cooks always do: She gave it to me without a second thought. And now I'm giving it to you. It takes a couple of days, but the time is almost all hands off and it's worth the wait. If you're a bread baker, I think you'll be impressed by how easy it is to get such a perfect result with so little work, and if you don't yet make bread, this is the place to start. The second time I had Mimi's version, she had swapped the rosemary for sweet onions. Either makes a wonderful snack for friends standing around the firepit, sitting beside the water with a glass of something in hand, or staring out over rolling hills on the cusp of a new season. **SERVES 16 TO 24**

In a measuring cup, combine the yeast, sugar, and ½ cup of the warm water and stir to dissolve. Let it sit for 5 or 6 minutes, until it foams and is alive (there's nothing more deflating than spending days on dough that doesn't work due to dead yeast).

(recipe continues)

Meanwhile, in a large bowl, combine the flour, kosher salt, and the remaining 3 cups warm water. Once the yeast mixture has proven itself to be happy and alive, add it to the bowl and stir until fully combined.

Pour 4 tablespoons of the olive oil into a very large lidded tub (I use an 8-quart lidded plastic tub but any large container you can seal will work) and swirl it around to coat the bottom and sides. Transfer the dough to the container, cover, and refrigerate for 2 days (in a pinch 1 day is okay, but I find the extra day makes a difference in the springiness of the final bread).

After the first day, you should see bubbles appear in the dough. It won't rise terribly high, but the bubbles mean it's working. After the second day, generously oil an 18 by 13-inch baking sheet and transfer the dough onto the sheet tray. Using your fingers, press out the dough evenly to fill the pan. It might resist a bit and you don't want to tear it, but keep pushing it until it's about 1 inch thick all over. Let the dough rise in a warm spot until it's very puffy and about twice its size with evident bubbles. This usually takes about 1½ hours in the summer but up to 2½ hours when it's colder. If it's chilly, I often turn on the light in my oven for a few minutes, then put the dough in the oven to rise, making sure to turn off the light when it goes in so it doesn't get too hot.

While the dough rises, heat about 2 tablespoons of the olive oil in a large sauté pan over medium-high heat. Add the onion and a sprinkle of sea salt and cook, stirring frequently, until the onion just begins to color and stick to the pan, 5 to 7 minutes. Add 2 or 3 tablespoons of water to the onion and continue to cook over medium heat until it is nicely caramelized, wilted, and the liquid has evaporated; set aside to cool slightly.

Preheat the oven to 450°F.

Once the dough is doubled in size, drizzle the top with the remaining 2 tablespoons of olive oil and, with oiled fingers, make indentations all over the dough until it's well dimpled. Spread the caramelized onions evenly over the top of the dough, then garnish with the thyme and a generous sprinkle of flaky salt. Bake for about 20 minutes, turning the pan once, until the top is beautifully golden brown all over. Let cool and either serve warm for the masses or cut into segments and freeze for later by wrapping the pieces in plastic wrap and then storing in a large plastic bag for up to 3 months.

Focaccia Crisps

Slab of focaccia
(see page 185)

This is a PS to the preceding recipe, a happy accident that came about in the midst of making this book. David, the darling husband of Kate, the photographer whose glorious, gorgeous light graces these pages, invented these crisps. One day after we finished shooting some of the images in the book you now hold in your hands, Kate took home a lonesome piece of the focaccia along with some leftover cheese and fig jam. David, his creative culinary sense firing much faster and sharper than ours after a long day, cut the focaccia into very thin pieces and toasted it—laden with olive oil as it is, the bread crisped up beautifully into slender crostini just right for smearing with a triple-crème Brie. So, thank you, David: For this idea, for sharing it with me, and, of course, for sharing Kate over more than a couple of weekends (and a holiday!) so that this book could exist.

Preheat the broiler.

Cut the focaccia into 3-inch squares, then slice the squares into ⅛-inch-thick slices. Transfer the slices to a baking sheet and toast for 2 or 3 minutes, turning once, until they are toasted and just golden. Watch them carefully so they don't burn. Remove from the oven, let cool, and serve.

Parmesan Grissini

¼ cup (56 grams)
unsalted butter

1 cup whole milk

1 teaspoon active
dry yeast

¼ teaspoon sugar

2⅔ cups (385 grams)
bread flour

2 teaspoons sea salt

½ cup (20 grams)
freshly grated
Parmesan

I started making a version of these in college when a friend gave me
his recipe, a scrawl of ingredients and rough amounts on the back
of an envelope. If I recall correctly, he'd just returned from a stint
studying in Italy and this was the souvenir he brought me. For years
I used the recipe he gave me to make long, knobby breadsticks that
I'd stand up in a mason jar to serve. But recently I began playing with
this old standby, and what you have here is an adaptation of that
original one. The basic idea is the same, but this version includes
some butter and a good bit of Parmesan, because, why not? Butter
and Parmesan make everything better. I still serve these in a tall jar
in the center of the table (if you've forgotten to pick up flowers, they
make a striking centerpiece). **MAKES ABOUT 30 GRISSINI**

Preheat the oven to 425°F. Line two baking sheets with parchment
paper.

In a small saucepan, melt the butter over low heat. Remove the
melted butter from the heat and add the milk. The mixture should be
just warm to the touch (about 110°F or roughly the feel of your skin's
temperature). Add the yeast and sugar and let the mixture sit until it
begins to foam, about 5 minutes.

In the bowl of a food processor, pulse the flour, salt, and
Parmesan to combine. Slowly pour in the yeast mixture and process
until the dough starts to come together. Continue to process for 3 to
4 minutes more (think of this as the kneading process—it takes some
time), until the dough pulls together into more of a ball (it won't
totally form a single lump, but it should be largely one piece with
some smaller bits bouncing along as well) and is very soft and smooth
to the touch, slightly elastic, and likely quite warm.

Transfer the dough to a work surface (no need to flour) and
stretch it into a rectangle, about 8 by 6 inches. Press your fingers into
the top of the dough to dimple it; you want to make indentations all
over the surface like a focaccia. Fold over the left third of the dough
and repeat the indentations on this folded section. Then fold over
the right third as you would a letter and use your fingers to make the
indentations again. Cover the folded dough with plastic wrap and let
rest on the counter for 30 minutes.

Using a pizza cutter or sharp knife, cut the dough into two pieces lengthwise. Use a rolling pin (no need for flour) to roll each piece into a large rectangle, about 8 by 10 inches. Then cut the dough widthwise into ½-inch strips (about 15 per piece).

Roll each strip back and forth on the work surface, starting at the center and moving your hands toward the ends, stretching the dough a bit as you roll it. Each one should be roughly 10 to 12 inches in length. Gently pinch the end of each strip, then place the strips on the prepared baking sheets to rest for another 10 minutes.

Transfer the baking sheets to the oven and bake for 12 to 14 minutes, rolling the grissini around after about 7 minutes to make sure they color on all sides. They are done when they are golden brown. Remove from the oven and let cool completely to crisp up before serving.

Carta di Musica
(Pane Carasau)

1 cup (140 grams) all-purpose flour, plus more for dusting and the work surface

1 cup (160 grams) semolina flour

2 teaspoons sea salt

½ cup and 2 tablespoons warm water

2 tablespoons extra-virgin olive oil, plus more for brushing

Flaky sea salt

These are a Sardinian treat: a chiffon-thin, crisp, shatteringly delicate cracker that looks as impressive as it tastes. I first discovered these ethereal crackers as carta di musica, so named because the crackers are as thin as the sheets of parchment that music is written on. But they are also referred to as pane carasau (toasted bread), because in the Sardinian language the verb *carasare* means "to toast." Either way, like biscotti, this ancient cracker was devised to last for a long time without needing any special preservation. How they used to get these crackers so thin as to be almost sheer was at first beyond me, as I tried rolling them every way imaginable and was stymied for a long time. Then I got canny and found the trick to a truly authentic carta di musica with a modern cheat: I use my pasta maker. It's clearly not traditional, but it does achieve an authentically brittle cracker that bubbles and blisters in the oven before being broken into shards perfectly suited for cheese, salumi, pâté, spreads, or even just on their own as an accompaniment to olives for aperitivo.

MAKES 12 LARGE PIECES OR MORE SMALL ONES

Place a baking sheet in the oven and preheat the oven to 500°F.

In a large bowl, combine both flours and the salt. Add the water and olive oil and stir until the mixture comes together to form a stiff dough. Knead the dough for 5 to 6 minutes, until very smooth; cover and let rest for 30 minutes.

Divide the dough into twelve or so pieces and cover with a clean kitchen towel so they don't dry out. Lightly dust one piece of the dough with all-purpose flour and flatten it to fit through the first level on your pasta maker. Continue working the dough through the machine to the thinnest level (I go to level 8), until the dough is nearly transparent. These crackers can get to be more than a foot in length so when they get unwieldy, cut them in half and continue working them through the machine.

(recipe continues)

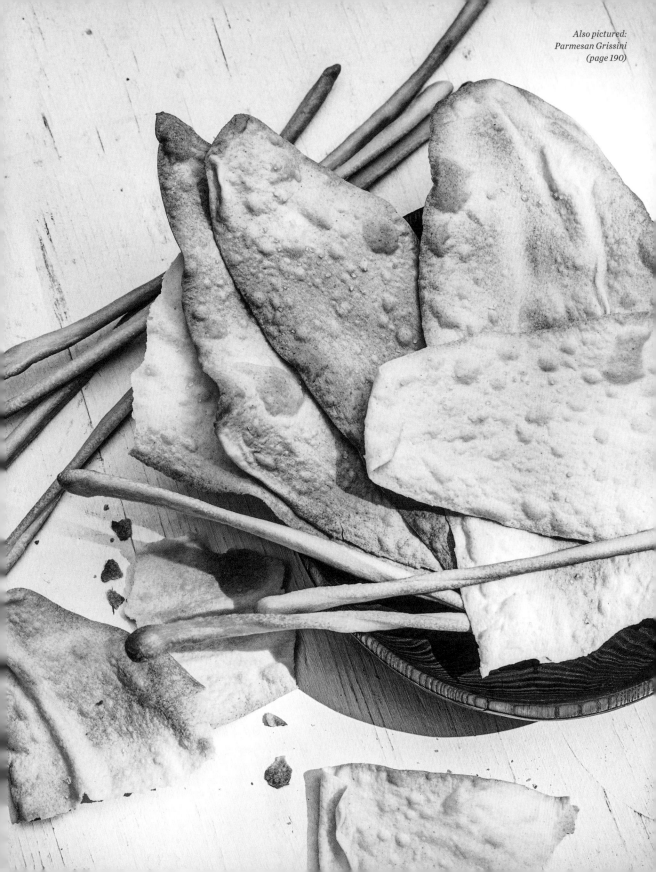

Also pictured:
Parmesan Grissini
(page 190)

If you don't have a pasta maker, roll out the dough by hand: On a lightly floured work surface, use a rolling pin to roll out each piece of dough as thinly as you can—they should be nearly paper thin. Don't worry about the shape, you want them to be organic, but try to get them as evenly rolled as possible.

When you've rolled out all the pieces, gently brush them with olive oil and sprinkle with some flaky salt.

To bake them, put as many as will fit directly on the hot baking sheet (probably two large). Bake about 3 minutes, or until they start to color and bubble. Using tongs, carefully flip them and continue to bake them for another 3 or so minutes, or until they've turned golden and brown on the edges and are blistered all over. Transfer to a wire rack to cool and repeat with the remaining dough. Serve these with cheese and charcuterie, alongside a salad, or simply on their own as a salty snack to accompany a glass of wine.

Middle Eastern–Style Flatbread

1 cup warm water

3 teaspoons active dry yeast

1 tablespoon sea salt

1 teaspoon sugar

3½ cups (490 grams) all-purpose flour, plus more for the work surface

¼ cup extra-virgin olive oil, for brushing

2 tablespoons za'atar (optional)

If you buy flatbread, pitas, or naan bread in the store, I implore you to do this: Look at the ingredients on the package the next time you're shopping. Rare is the packaged flatbread that doesn't have a long list of ingredients, many unidentifiable and unpronounceable. All of which is suspect because good-quality bread needs no more than what you see here to be perfect. The other ingredients that are stabilizing, preserving, and softening the packaged stuff are unnecessary if you're willing to do just a little bit of work and have quite a bit of fun at the same time. These flatbreads do require a couple of hours to rise and some light kneading along the way, but what you'll be rewarded with are tender, toothsome, and lightly charred breads for dipping (try with Bessara with Harissa on page 127) or topping (Spiced Lamb Flatbreads with Lemony Hummus on page 168). They also freeze really well. MAKES ABOUT 12 FLATBREADS

In a measuring cup, combine the water, yeast, salt, and sugar and stir to dissolve. Let this mixture sit for 5 or 6 minutes, until it begins to foam on top.

In a large bowl, stir together the flour and frothy yeast mixture. When the dough has fully come together, knead it until it's soft and elastic, about 5 minutes. Cover the bowl with plastic wrap and put it in a warm spot for an hour or two, until it's almost doubled in size. On a warm day, this might only take an hour, but it might be considerably longer if cool out. (If it's chilly, I often turn on the light in my oven for a few minutes while I mix the dough. Then I put the bowl in the oven to rise, making sure to turn off the light when the bowl goes in so it doesn't get too hot and overproof.)

When the dough has risen, punch it down, divide it into twelve pieces, and roll them around to make small balls, covering them as you do this so the dough doesn't dry out. Working with one ball at a time, use a rolling pin to flatten each piece into a 4- to 6-inch round. These rounds will be very organic in shape, and that's fine—don't aim for perfection here. Stack the rolled flatbreads with parchment paper

(recipe continues)

between each piece to keep them from sticking together while you roll out the rest of the dough.

Put the olive oil in one small bowl and the za'atar (if using) in another.

Preheat a grill or set a large cast-iron skillet over high heat.

When the grill or the pan is hot, lightly brush one side of a bread with olive oil and place the oiled side directly on the grates or the bottom of the pan. While it cooks, brush the top of the bread with olive oil. Cook for about 2 minutes or until the bread begins to bubble and char a bit. Flip and continue to cook until nicely browned and puffy, about another 2 minutes. Remove from the heat and sprinkle with the za'atar. Keep the breads warm in foil until ready to serve or let cool completely, then freeze in plastic wrap for up to 3 months. To rewarm, defrost the breads, wrap them in foil, and heat in a 300°F oven for about 10 minutes.

Savory Cheddar Madeleines

½ cup (70 grams) all-purpose flour

¼ cup (40 grams) cornmeal

2 teaspoons sugar

½ teaspoon baking powder

¾ teaspoon sea salt

2 large eggs, beaten

5 tablespoons (70 grams) melted butter, plus more for the pan

1 cup (40 grams) finely grated Cheddar

2 to 3 tablespoons whole milk

It's hard to talk about madeleines without the obvious reference to Proust, but these are not related in any way to my past. They are instead a cute, fun, cheesy little snack that I made because I wanted something for my friend Erica's kids to enjoy but with a bit of a sophisticated twist (meaning if the kids didn't like them, I hoped everyone else would). Madeleines are traditionally sweet, so my thought was this: If they look like something from a bakery window who wouldn't want to try one? The polenta nods to cornbread and the Cheddar flavor is very present, so while they look like little French pastries, they're really more like savory muffins.

MAKES ABOUT 3 DOZEN

Preheat the oven to 375°F. Butter a mini-madeleine pan and set aside. (If you don't have a madeleine pan, a mini-muffin tin will work.)

In a large bowl, combine the flour, cornmeal, sugar, baking powder, and salt and mix well. Add the eggs and mix until you have a thick batter. Mix in the melted butter and Cheddar until fully incorporated. Add 2 tablespoons of the milk and mix until combined. You want the batter to drop easily from a spoon, like a cake batter, so if it's a bit thick, add the remaining 1 tablespoon milk and mix again.

Drop a teaspoon of the batter into the center of each madeleine cup, taking care not to fill each cup more than two-thirds full. Transfer the pan to the oven and bake for 7 to 9 minutes, until the madeleines have puffed in the middle and are beginning to brown on the edges. Remove from the pan and serve warm.

Tarallini

¼ cup dry white wine, warmed

¼ cup warm water, plus 2 tablespoons

1 teaspoon active dry yeast

½ teaspoon sugar

2 cups (280 grams) all-purpose flour

1½ teaspoons sea salt

¼ cup extra-virgin olive oil

Think of these as Italian potato chips. They're salty, crunchy, and exactly what you want with a glass of wine or a beer. Originally from Puglia, Italy, tarallini are traditionally an unleavened snack made from just four ingredients. And while the main ingredients are nearly always the same (as is the cooking process of boiling them first, as you do bagels or pretzels, before baking them), the proportions vary widely from recipe to recipe. My version departs from the classic in that I've added yeast and a short rest to the method, which I find gives them a lighter, crunchier texture. You can, of course, add additional flavorings if you like (fennel, red chile, and black pepper all being classic combinations), but I prefer them very simple and small— taralli, which you see more commonly packaged, are about three to four inches in diameter, whereas I make these tarallini closer to an inch or two. MAKES ABOUT 60

In a measuring cup, combine the warm wine and water (they should be about 110°F or roughly the feel of your skin's temperature), yeast, and sugar and stir to dissolve. Let this mixture sit for 5 or 6 minutes, until it begins to foam on top.

Meanwhile, put the flour and salt in the bowl of a food processor. Add the olive oil to the yeast mixture, turn on the machine, and slowly pour in the yeast mixture and process until the dough starts to come together. Continue to process for 10 to 15 minutes more (think of this as the kneading process—it takes some time) until the dough begins to pull together and is very soft and smooth to the touch, slightly elastic, and likely quite warm. It won't form a single lump, but it should be largely one piece with some smaller bits bouncing along as well.

Form the dough into a slightly flattened oval and transfer it to an oiled bowl. Cover with plastic wrap and let rest for 1 hour. The dough should puff a bit but will not double in size.

Preheat the oven to 350°F. Bring a large pot of salted water to a boil.

(recipe continues)

Cut off pieces of the dough and shape the tarallini by rolling the pieces into ¼-inch-thick strips about 2 inches in length. Shape the strips into small rounds and join them at the bottom by pressing the ends together. Place them on a piece of parchment until they've all been shaped. Don't worry if they're not perfect rounds; they should have a handmade look to them.

Once you've shaped all the dough, use a slotted spoon to lower them into the boiling water, working in batches so as not to overcrowd the pot. Let them cook for 20 to 30 seconds. They're done when they float to the surface on their own. Use a slotted spoon to remove them from the water and transfer them to a clean dish towel to dry while you continue to boil the remaining dough.

Once all the tarallini have been boiled, transfer them to a baking sheet and bake in the oven for about 30 minutes, until just golden brown on top. Let the tarallini cool completely before serving.

Gluten-Free Fennel Crackers

¾ cup (85 grams) almond flour

½ cup (95 grams) potato starch

½ teaspoon sugar

¼ teaspoon sea salt

1 teaspoon fennel seeds, lightly crushed

¼ teaspoon freshly ground black pepper

1 large egg

2 tablespoons extra-virgin olive oil

Pinch of flaky sea salt

Some people are gluten-free; I'm decidedly on the gluten-rich side of things. However, I have a lot of friends who, either because of health issues or lifestyle choices, do not share my affinity, and as such, these are made, with love, for them. And while I know there are a lot of options available these days for gluten-free folks, I wanted a cracker so good that even those of us who didn't want to eliminate gluten would enjoy them. PS: You could easily substitute an herb here instead of fennel for a variation. I think rosemary or thyme would be great, but don't skip the flaky salt on top. MAKES ABOUT 36 CRACKERS

Preheat the oven to 375°F. Line a baking sheet with parchment paper.

In a large bowl, combine the almond flour, potato starch, sugar, salt, fennel seeds, and pepper and mix well. Add the egg and olive oil and, using a fork at first, stir together to begin to create a dough. When the dough has partially come together but isn't fully combined, use your hands to knead the dough until all the dry ingredients are integrated and you have a slightly sticky, cohesive ball.

Place a sheet of parchment paper on a work surface and lay the ball in the middle. Flatten the ball and place a sheet of parchment paper on top. Use a rolling pin to roll the dough between the two parchment sheets until the dough is quite thin—between ⅛ inch and ¼ inch thick. Gently remove the top sheet of parchment. Using a pizza cutter or a knife, cut the dough into rectangles or squares, about 2 inches long (some of the shapes may break; just put them aside to reroll with your scraps).

Carefully transfer the rectangles to the prepared baking sheet, sprinkle with flaky salt, and bake for 10 to 12 minutes, or until the crackers are golden and just beginning to color slightly on the edges.

Meanwhile, press any dough scraps into a ball and repeat the rolling and cutting process. This dough doesn't have much fat in it, so it won't get tough when rolled repeatedly; feel free to use up all the dough by rolling the scraps after each cutting.

Socca, Four Ways

Socca, for the uninitiated, is a chickpea flour pancake originally from Nice, France. As thin as a crepe, socca are cooked on the stove and then topped and reheated as you would a pizza. Made from legumes, these pancakes are inherently gluten-free (a plus for some) and utterly delicious (a plus for all). Like crepes, socca batter benefits from a rest before being cooked so the liquid can be fully absorbed by the flour, and the first pancake will likely not be the prettiest (it's just the warm-up, so don't fret, the rest will be gorgeous). I make a full batch of socca (they freeze, layered between parchment paper really well, so you can keep them on hand all the time) and then make them with a variety of toppings. The ideas below are a few of my favorites, but like a pizza crust, socca is really a tabula rasa for whatever inspires you. **SERVES 4 TO 6**

Socca

2 cups (220 grams) chickpea flour

1 teaspoon sea salt

2 cups lukewarm water

¼ cup extra-virgin olive oil, plus more for frying

Freshly ground black pepper

In a medium bowl, combine the flour and salt, then gradually pour in the water. Add the olive oil, season with salt and pepper, and whisk well. Cover and let the mixture rest for at least 20 minutes and up to 2 hours in the fridge.

Set a 10-inch nonstick skillet over medium-high heat and add enough olive oil to just coat the bottom of the pan. When the oil shimmers, ladle about ¾ cup of the batter into the skillet, tipping the pan gently in a circular motion to make sure the batter is evenly distributed. Lower the heat to medium and cook until the batter begins to crisp at the edges, about 3 minutes. Using a thin spatula (I like to use an offset or fish spatula for this), carefully flip the socca and cook for another 2 to 3 minutes, until it's golden on both sides. Remove the socca to a baking sheet and repeat with the remaining batter.

When all the socca have been cooked, you can begin to assemble the various toppings or let the socca cool completely and freeze them, separated by pieces of parchment, in a zip-top bag.

(recipe continues)

1 head garlic

Extra-virgin olive oil
for drizzling

1 small zucchini or
yellow squash (or a
combination), sliced

Sea salt and freshly
ground black pepper

⅓ cup ricotta cheese

6 to 8 red or yellow
cherry tomatoes,
quartered

Fresh basil for garnish

Flaky sea salt (optional)

RICOTTA WITH ROASTED GARLIC, SUMMER SQUASH, AND CHERRY TOMATOES

Preheat the oven to 400°F.

Cut the top off the garlic head to expose the flesh of the cloves. Place the head in the center of a piece of aluminum foil, drizzle the top of the garlic with olive oil, a tablespoon or so just to moisten it, and then bundle the garlic in the foil so it's completely enclosed. Put the garlic on a baking sheet, transfer to the oven, and cook until it's fragrant and very soft, 45 minutes. To check, carefully open the foil pouch and press on the exposed garlic with a paring knife—if it's still a bit firm, reseal the foil and continue cooking for another 15 minutes or so.

Meanwhile, place the squash on a baking sheet and drizzle lightly with oil. Sprinkle with salt and pepper and toss to coat everything well. Transfer the pan to the oven (ideally above the garlic so it browns nicely) and cook, turning once, until the squash are tender and beginning to color, 10 to 12 minutes. Remove and set aside.

When the garlic is done, remove from the oven but leave the oven on. Let the garlic cool until you can handle it, then squeeze out the flesh of the cloves into a small airtight container. At this point you want to separate out 2 or 3 cloves for the socca and freeze the remainder to use later.

Line a baking sheet with parchment paper and place the soccas on the prepared sheet. In a small bowl, use a fork to mash together the ricotta with 2 or 3 roasted garlic cloves. Spread the ricotta mixture over the top of the soccas, then top with the roasted squash and quartered tomatoes. Place the soccas in the oven for about 5 minutes, or until the ricotta begins to melt and the vegetables are warmed through. Before serving, garnish with basil leaves and, if desired, a sprinkle of flaky salt.

About 6 tablespoons
extra-virgin olive oil

½ sweet onion (Vidalia),
thinly sliced into half-
moons

Sea salt and freshly
ground black pepper

4 to 6 trumpet or other
mushrooms, trimmed
and sliced lengthwise

4 to 6 asparagus spears,
trimmed

1 or 2 handfuls of
arugula

3 ounces fresh
mozzarella, torn
into bite-size pieces

CARAMELIZED ONIONS WITH MOZZARELLA, ARUGULA, ASPARAGUS, AND TRUMPET MUSHROOMS

In a large skillet, heat 2 tablespoons of olive oil over medium heat. When the oil shimmers, add the onion and cook, stirring frequently, until the onion begins to soften, about 5 minutes. If the pan seems too dry, add a tablespoon more of the olive oil. Season the onion with salt and pepper, lower the heat to medium-low, and continue cooking, stirring frequently, until the onion begins to color, another 5 to 7 minutes. Remove the onion from the pan and let cool.

Using the same pan (no need to wipe it out), heat another 2 tablespoons of olive oil over medium-high. When the oil is hot, reduce the heat to medium and add the mushrooms. Sprinkle with salt and pepper and cook for about 5 minutes. Give the mushrooms a turn and continue cooking until they start to brown. If you're using trumpet mushrooms, they won't release very much liquid so the cooking time should be about 10 minutes total. If you're using cremini, baby bella, or another type, they will release considerable liquid so be sure to cook them until the juices have had time to evaporate and the mushrooms brown a bit. Turn off the heat but leave the pan on the warm burner.

Meanwhile, bring a medium pot of salted water to a boil. Blanch the asparagus until just crisp-tender. The spears are ready when they turn bright green and the water returns to a boil. Drain the asparagus in a colander and run under cold water to stop the cooking process. Cut into 2-inch pieces. Add the asparagus and arugula to the pan with the mushrooms. Toss all the vegetables together in the still-warm pan just to wilt the arugula and lightly coat everything in the oil (add a bit more oil if it seems too dry).

Preheat the oven to 400°F. Line a baking sheet with parchment paper.

Place the soccas on the prepared baking sheet. Spread a couple tablespoons of the caramelized onions on top of the soccas and scatter the mozzarella over that. Evenly layer the vegetable mixture over the cheese, then transfer to the oven for 5 minutes, or until the mozzarella has melted fully.

(recipe continues)

3 tablespoons extra-
virgin olive oil

1 garlic clove, smashed

1 cup bread crumbs,
preferably homemade

¼ teaspoon red pepper
flakes, or to taste

Sea salt and freshly
ground black pepper

3 to 4 sprigs flat-leaf
parsley, leaves picked
and roughly chopped,
plus more for garnish

Zest of 1 lemon

½ cup Harissa-Roasted
Tomatoes (page 75) or
spicy tomato sauce of
your choice

One 4-ounce tin
good-quality sardines
in oil, drained

SARDINES WITH HARISSA-ROASTED TOMATOES AND PANGRATTATO

To make the pangrattato, heat the olive oil in a large skillet over medium heat. Add the garlic and cook until just fragrant, about 1 minute. Add the bread crumbs and red pepper flakes and season with salt and black pepper. Lower the heat to medium-low and continue to cook, stirring frequently to keep the crumbs from burning, until they are golden brown and beginning to crisp, 10 to 12 minutes. Remove from the heat and pull out and discard the garlic clove. Mix the parsley and lemon zest into the bread crumbs. Season as needed with a bit more salt and black pepper and set aside. The pangrattato will continue to crisp up as it cools.

Preheat the oven to 400°F. Line a baking sheet with parchment paper.

Place the soccas on the prepared baking sheet. Evenly spread the roasted tomatoes on top of the soccas and top with the sardines, then transfer to the oven for 3 to 4 minutes, until the tomatoes are just warmed through. Remove from the oven and generously sprinkle with the pangrattato. Garnish with parsley, then serve.

TALEGGIO WITH MARINATED ARTICHOKES AND PROSCIUTTO

3 ounces Taleggio
cheese, rind removed,
cut into bite-size pieces

½ cup Marinated Baby
Artichokes (page 76),
with their marinating
liquid, or store-bought

3 to 4 slices prosciutto,
roughly torn

Extra-virgin olive oil for
drizzling

Fresh basil for garnish

Preheat the oven to 400°F. Line a baking sheet with parchment
paper.

Place the soccas on the prepared baking sheet. Top the soccas
evenly with the cheese and the artichokes, then transfer to the oven
for about 5 minutes or until the cheese has just melted.

Drape the prosciutto over the top of the soccas and drizzle with a
tiny bit of olive oil (or, if you've made your own marinated artichokes,
use the tangy marinating liquid). Garnish generously with basil,
then serve.

Chapter 8

A SWEET
SPOONFUL

I DON'T HAVE MUCH OF A SWEET TOOTH, but what I do have leans toward fruit-centric confections. Apricots, cherries, peaches, and any stone fruit are really my first instinct, followed quickly by lemon anything. It's the variation in Mother Nature's flavors and the endless combinations proffered up by crumbles, cobblers, tarts, crisps, and crostatas that get me.

Chocolate comes in second when I think of dessert. I really like chocolate. I just don't think you need very much of it. However, I am totally accustomed to being told I'm wrong on this count, as I'm married to, and the sibling of, chocolate devotees. In the case of Ken, if left to his own devices, he will always go for the chocolate option on the menu, so that usually works out pretty well if we're sharing (at least for me). I get a bite or two, and he gets, well, less than he'd like. With regard to my sister, upon sharing a recipe for a fruit tart or cake with her, I inevitably get this response: "Wow! That sounds great! Can I make it with chocolate instead?" So while I care for chocolate, I don't crave it like some. But I do find myself baking a lot of chocolate desserts for the sake of the humans closest to me.

The other flavor that does me in when done well is vanilla—not as in ice cream, but as in fresh from the bean and infused or added to almost everything. When blended with cream, mixed with fruit, or added to chocolate, the flavor of real vanilla permeates and adds dimension—there's nothing plain about it. The aroma, gentle but apparent, can be almost intoxicating at first wisp, followed by the flavor, which is distinct but subtle, floral, and creamy.

Taken together, fruit, chocolate, and vanilla are the essential ingredients I think of when I think of sweets that I want to eat—and they are what you'll find in the coming pages. I also think small. My belief, and again I acknowledge this is not something universally agreed upon, is that less is better when it comes to dessert. A small cup, a thin slice, a spoonful or two is all you really need, just enough to leave you smiling.

A single biscotti, a square of cake, a tiny glass of custard, a miniature ice-cream sandwich—each of these recipes has something that makes them special, a little different, but the commonality in all of them is that they are meant to be served, and savored, small. Of course, if you are a die-hard dessert person and find my whole "less is better" approach preposterous, please feel free to ignore me and double the serving size for each recipe.

Rhubarb-Plum Cobbler Cake (page 231)

Chocolate Zucchini Snacking Cakes

2 large eggs

1½ cups (300 grams) lightly packed dark brown sugar

¾ cup extra-virgin olive oil

1 tablespoon pure vanilla extract

2 cups packed grated zucchini (about 2 small or 1 large zucchini)

1 cup (140 grams) all-purpose flour

¾ cup (95 grams) whole-wheat flour

⅔ cup (55 grams) unsweetened cocoa powder

1 teaspoon baking powder

1 teaspoon baking soda

1 teaspoon sea salt

1 cup (170 grams) semisweet chocolate chips

½ cup shredded sweetened coconut (optional)

2 tablespoons demerara sugar

If you're a vegetable gardener (and if you're not yet, maybe this cake will convince you to try), you know that come September the sheer quantity of zucchini you get from just one vine is bonkers. Like cucumbers, once they get going zucchini plants are true givers, and I usually find myself with far more than I know what to do with. This snacking cake is an irresistible way to make good use of some of those late-summer squash. And, while I'm the last person to hide my vegetables under a cloak of chocolate, with the zucchini, olive oil, and whole-wheat flour here, I do feel like I'm veering toward something akin to a healthy snack, no matter how deceptively decadent it tastes. I use mini-panettone paper cups for these cakes (2⅜ by 2 inches), but you could bake it in a loaf pan as well and simply extend the cooking time accordingly (about 1 hour). **MAKES ABOUT 12 CAKES**

Preheat the oven to 325°F. Place twelve paper baking cups on a baking sheet with at least 3 inches between them and set aside.

In a large bowl, beat together the eggs, brown sugar, olive oil, and vanilla until it is glossy and well combined, about 3 minutes. Fold the grated zucchini into the mixture and set aside.

In a medium bowl, sift together both flours, the cocoa, baking powder, baking soda, and salt. Add the dry ingredients to the zucchini mixture and stir gently until it's all uniform and no traces of the flour-cocoa mixture are visible. Stir in the chocolate chips and, if using, the coconut, evenly distributing.

Transfer the batter to the baking cups, filling them two-thirds of the way up the sides. Sprinkle each evenly with the demerara sugar and transfer the pan to the oven. Bake the cakes for 30 to 35 minutes, until a skewer inserted into the center comes out nearly clean with just a few crumbs clinging to it. Remove from the oven and transfer the cakes to a wire rack to cool completely before serving.

Double Chocolate Olive Oil Biscotti

2 cups (280 grams)
all-purpose flour

¾ cup plus
2 tablespoons cocoa
powder (70 grams),
plus more for dusting

1 teaspoon sea salt

1 teaspoon baking soda

1¾ cups (350 grams)
lightly packed dark
brown sugar

⅓ cup (65 grams)
granulated sugar

3 tablespoons
extra-virgin olive oil

1 tablespoon pure
vanilla extract

3 large eggs

1 cup (170 grams)
semisweet chocolate
chips

2 tablespoons
demerara sugar

It's only in the past few years that I've integrated olive oil so prominently into my baking, and I credit two people with this turn of events: Diana Henry, the doyenne of cookery in my opinion, and my husband, Ken. Diana started my veer toward olive oil baking with her impossibly perfect, life-affirming chocolate olive oil cake from *How to Eat a Peach* (make it, trust me). Ken further inspired my exploration when he received a higher-than-desirable cholesterol reading. In an attempt to remedy his levels without forgoing sweets, I started playing with how and where I could swap olive oil for butter without anyone noticing the difference; biscotti works brilliantly. MAKES ABOUT 40

Preheat the oven to 350°F. Line two baking sheets with parchment paper and set aside.

Sift the flour, cocoa, salt, and baking soda together into a medium bowl and set aside.

In a large bowl, mix together the brown sugar, granulated sugar, and olive oil with a silicone spatula. Stir in the vanilla and then add the eggs one at a time, mixing after each addition.

Add a third of the flour mixture to the bowl with the sugars and mix well. Continue with the remaining flour mixture until it's blended and the dough is sticky. Mix in the chocolate chips.

Dust a clean work surface lightly with cocoa powder. Divide the dough in two and work each piece into a 2 by 10-inch log. Carefully transfer the logs to one of the prepared baking sheets. Gently flatten them with your hand. Sprinkle each log with 1 tablespoon of the demerara sugar and transfer to the oven.

Bake until the biscotti have spread slightly and are beginning to crack on top, 30 to 40 minutes. Remove from the oven and let cool for about 15 minutes. Lower the oven to 325°F.

When the biscotti are cool enough to handle, cut them on the bias into ½-inch slices. Place each slice cut side down on the baking sheets (you'll need the second one at this point to hold all the biscotti) and bake for another 15 to 20 minutes, until crisp and a bit dry. Store in an airtight container at room temperature for up to 2 weeks.

Almond and Orange Lace Sandwich Cookies

½ cup (112 grams) unsalted butter

½ cup (100 grams) sugar

1 tablespoon all-purpose flour

¼ teaspoon sea salt

¾ cup (84 grams) almond flour

2 tablespoons whole milk

1 teaspoon almond extract

Zest of 1 orange

6 ounces (170 grams) semisweet or dark chocolate, melted

There are recipes that seem complicated because they are; they have lots of ingredients or require complex techniques. Then there are recipes that seem as though they *should be* complicated but in fact are not. This is one of those recipes. Lace cookies have a delicacy that makes you think there's some special pastry-chef trick to making them. They have a toasty maple flavor that leads you to believe the ingredients are slightly unusual. None of this is true. These lace cookies are quite easy to make if you follow the recipe: Let the batter cool sufficiently before shaping and keep your eyes on them in the oven so they don't get too dark. They also combine a few common ingredients—almond flour and orange zest—that conspire to taste much more exotic than you would imagine they should. They are the kind of cookie that people find slightly dazzling; the uninitiated might even suspect you've bought them at a fancy bakery. Imagine their delight when you disabuse them of this notion. MAKES 18 TO 20

Preheat the oven to 350°F. Line two half baking sheets with silicone mats.

In a medium saucepan, melt the butter over medium heat. When the butter is bubbling, add the sugar, all-purpose flour, and salt and whisk until the sugar dissolves and the mixture is cohesive, 3 to 4 minutes.

Add the almond flour and milk and continue stirring until smooth and a bit thicker. Remove the pan from the heat and stir in the almond extract and orange zest. Let the batter cool for about 15 minutes so it can set up a bit.

Using a teaspoon measure, scoop the batter onto the prepared baking sheets, leaving at least 3 inches between each dollop. Bake the cookies for about 7 minutes, or until just browning around the edges. Let the cookies cool until they are firm enough to be carefully transferred to a cooling rack, about 5 minutes.

When the cookies are thoroughly cooled, use a small offset spatula to spread the melted chocolate on the underside of one cookie before topping it with a second cookie to make sandwiches. Repeat with the remaining cookies. Let the chocolate set up before serving. Store cookies in an airtight container for up to 2 weeks.

Also pictured: Double Chocolate
Olive Oil Biscotti (page 215)

Salted Silver-Dollar Ice Cream Sandwiches

¾ cup (105 grams) all-purpose flour, plus more for the work surface

¼ cup plus 2 tablespoons (35 grams) unsweetened cocoa powder

½ cup (100 grams) sugar

⅛ teaspoon sea salt

⅛ teaspoon baking soda

7 tablespoons (98 grams) unsalted butter, cut into pieces

2 tablespoons whole milk

1 teaspoon pure vanilla extract

Flaky sea salt for sprinkling

Ice cream for filling (I'm partial to vanilla, malted milk, and mint chip)

A sprinkle of salt on dark chocolate takes this cookie from a simple wafer to something slightly more grown-up. And when two of these cookies surround a small scoop of your favorite ice cream, it's the kind of dessert that will make snackers of all ages smile. I make these in a couple of flavors, on the assumption that people will want more than one, and because when it comes to most things, everyone has different tastes and opinions. As the old adage goes, "That's why they make chocolate and vanilla ice cream." **MAKES ABOUT 40 COOKIES FOR 20 SANDWICHES**

In the bowl of a food processor, pulse the flour, cocoa, sugar, salt, and baking soda to combine. Add the butter and pulse again until a coarse meal forms. Add the milk and vanilla and let the machine run until the dough rides around on the blade, about 2 minutes. Transfer the dough to a lightly floured work surface and knead it until it comes together fully. Form the dough into a flat disk, wrap it in plastic wrap, and chill until it's set, at least 1 hour (you can also freeze the dough for up to 3 months to use later).

Preheat the oven to 350°F. Line two baking sheets with parchment paper.

Take the dough from the fridge and give it a minute to soften so you can roll it. Place the dough between two pieces of parchment and roll it out until it's about ¼ inch thick. Using a round 2-inch cookie cutter, cut out the dough and put the cookies on the prepared baking sheets leaving about 1 inch between them. If you'd like, use a fork to dock the cookies by gently pressing the tines into the top of each to make a couple of rows. Sprinkle the cookies lightly with some flaky salt and transfer to the oven. Bake the cookies for 8 to 10 minutes, until they puff slightly and sink again. Once the first round of cookies are in the oven, press the scrap dough back into a ball and roll it out again to make more cookies (continue doing this until you use up all the dough). Remove the cookies from the oven and transfer to a wire rack to thoroughly cool before filling. The cookies will continue to crisp up as they sit.

Let your ice cream sit at room temperature for about 10 minutes, or until it's easily scoopable. Lay half the cookies top side down and, with a small ice cream scoop, place about 2 tablespoons ice cream on each of these cookies. Top the ice cream with the remaining cookies, top side up, and press down gently to form sandwiches. Use a small offset spatula to smooth the sides of the sandwiches. Transfer the sandwiches to a baking sheet and place in the freezer to set up fully, about 20 to 30 minutes, before serving.

Chocolate Pots
with Boozy Cream

2 cups heavy cream, divided

1 vanilla bean, split lengthwise, seeds scraped and pod reserved

5 ounces (¼ cup and 1 tablespoon) whole milk

6 ounces bittersweet chocolate (60% or 70% cacao), chopped

3 large egg yolks

2½ tablespoons confectioners' sugar

2 to 3 tablespoons brandy or other liqueur of your choice

When I was about ten years old, my parents took my sister and me on a trip to Europe. One night, after a rather bumpy ferry ride from Dover to Calais, we found ourselves in a small hotel restaurant called Chez Edouard. After a long day of travel, our dinner consisted of what I remember to be a mountain of french fries, salty and crispy and light and thin, followed by a small glass dish of chocolate mousse topped with a spoonful of whipped cream. It was the dreamiest of dinners for a sleepy eight- and ten-year-old. To this day I can summon the taste of those authentically *French* fries. But as I've gotten older, my adoration for chocolate mousse has morphed into something slightly more mature. Almost vibrating with intense chocolate flavor, these little pots are that thing. Cooked stovetop before being baked at low heat in a bain-marie (water bath), these little cups are baked slowly until a rich, dark top layer forms over the silky, dense custard inside. Unlike the fluffy, airy mousse I recall from France years ago, this is a grown-ups' dessert—made more so by the addition of some booze-spiked whipped cream to counterbalance the chocolate. I use whatever liqueur I have—Godiva, Amaretto, Cointreau, even a splash of whiskey won't go awry depending on your taste. But know this: Even if you love chocolate (and I live with someone whose mantra when it comes to dessert is "Chocolate never goes out of season"), you'll want to make these quite small lest you send your guests into a chocolate frenzy. They really are that rich.

MAKES SIX 3-OUNCE CHOCOLATE POTS

Preheat the oven to 275°F.

In a small saucepan, heat 1 cup of the cream and the vanilla bean seeds and pod over medium-low heat. When the cream is just warm, give it a stir, then remove from the heat and cover. Let steep for about 20 minutes.

Meanwhile, in another small saucepan, combine the milk and chocolate over medium heat and cook, stirring, until the chocolate is melted. Remove from the heat.

(recipe continues)

Also pictured: Vanilla-Lemon Posset with Stone Fruit Compote (page 227) and Almond and Orange Lace Sandwich Cookies (page 218)

In a medium bowl, whisk the egg yolks with $1\frac{1}{2}$ tablespoons of the sugar until thoroughly combined. Remove the vanilla pod from the cream mixture and discard. Slowly spoon a bit of the vanilla cream into the eggs to temper them (you don't want to cook the eggs) and stir. Stir the remaining vanilla cream and the chocolate milk into the eggs. When the mixture is well blended, place a fine-mesh sieve over a large glass measuring cup and strain it.

Prepare a water bath (bain-marie) by placing a roasting pan or other high-sided oven-safe pan on a baking sheet and bringing a kettle of water to a boil. Place six or eight small ramekins (depending on the size you have, you may need more or less) in the prepared pan. Pour the chocolate custard into the ramekins and transfer the pan to the heated oven. Pour the boiling water into the pan so it surrounds the ramekins and comes about halfway up their sides—be careful not to splash the water in the custard. Bake the custards in the water bath until the tops puff slightly, 50 minutes to 1 hour.

Remove the pan from the oven, again taking care not to splash water into the custard. Remove the pots from the hot water and let cool for at least a few hours to fully set. You can serve them now (they are wonderfully silky at room temperature) or transfer them to the fridge. Make sure to let them come back to room temperature before serving. (Note: Don't cover the pots with plastic wrap until they're fully cooled or you'll get condensation that will drip on the tops.)

Just before serving, put the remaining 1 cup cream in the bowl of a stand mixer (or use a hand mixer if you like) to whip it. Add the remaining 1 tablespoon sugar and, when soft peaks have formed, the booze. Continue whipping until the cream reaches your desired consistency (I like medium-stiff peaks here). Spoon some of the whipped cream on top of each custard before serving.

Vanilla-Lemon Posset with Stone Fruit Compote

2 cups heavy cream

¾ cup (150 grams) sugar, plus 1 tablespoon, plus more as needed

1 vanilla bean, split lengthwise, seeds scraped and pod reserved

5 tablespoons freshly squeezed lemon juice

2 tablespoons water

2 apriums, pluots, apricots, plums, peaches, or a combination, halved, pitted, and cut into ½-inch wedges

This has everything I look for in a dessert: It's rich but not saccharine. It comes together in minutes and sets up quickly (a couple of hours are all you need for the lemon juice to thicken the cream). And it features what I believe to be two of the most delectable flavors known to humankind: lemon and vanilla. I make these quite small—about a quarter cup per serving—as I'm a big believer in leaving people wanting more rather than overdoing it. I also love to balance out the creaminess of the posset with a spoonful of something fruity on top. With all the new hybrid stone fruit available now, I've fallen hard for apriums and pluots for this one, but you can use any stone fruit, really. Plus, after I scrape the vanilla bean seeds into the posset, I add the leftover pod to the compote to infuse it as well for a double hit of that heady vanilla flavor. SERVES 8

In a medium saucepan, bring the cream, ¾ cup of the sugar, and the vanilla bean seeds to a boil, stirring to dissolve the sugar. Once the mixture begins to bubble, lower the heat and let simmer for 3 minutes. Remove from the heat and stir in the lemon juice. Let sit for about 10 minutes for the flavors to meld.

Strain the mixture through a fine-mesh sieve into a large glass measuring cup and then pour into eight small glasses, jars, or cups. Let cool completely (if you don't, the top will wrinkle), then cover with plastic wrap and chill until fully set, at least 4 hours.

Meanwhile, in a small saucepan, heat the water, 1 tablespoon of the sugar, the cut fruit, and the vanilla bean pod over medium heat. Stir the mixture until the sugar dissolves and the fruit releases its juices and begins to soften but not totally fall apart, 6 to 8 minutes. Remove and discard the vanilla bean pod. Taste the compote and add a bit more sugar if you think it needs it. Let cool. When ready to serve, top the chilled possets with a small spoonful of the compote.

Tangy Lemon Tartlets

12 tablespoons (168 grams) unsalted butter, at room temperature, divided

⅓ cup (40 grams) confectioners' sugar

3 large egg yolks

½ teaspoon sea salt

1¼ cups (175 grams) all-purpose flour

2 large eggs

½ cup (100 grams) granulated sugar

½ cup freshly squeezed lemon juice

When I was growing up in California, citrus trees were an unexceptional part of the landscape. Mexican limes, Meyer lemons, Kalamansi, juicing oranges—there they were in our yard, as unremarkable to my eyes as apple trees might be to a New Englander. But now that I live on the East Coast, the thought of lemons and limes within arm's reach (not to mention available all year long) is both magical and enviable. Which is, I think, why lemon desserts are so alluring to me—citrus is what home tastes like. These tiny tarts feature a lemon curd made in the style of French sabayon, by gradually thickening egg yolks, sugar, and lemon juice together over a pan set above boiling water. The crust I like for this snack is pâte sablée, a very delicate and buttery pastry that's barely sweetened, so the brightness of the lemon custard isn't muted by a sugary crust. Together, the combination of the delicate cookie-like crust and the tangy, buttery curd conspire to be French in consistency and Californian in flavor.

Note: I use perforated silicone tart rings and a perforated baking mat in this recipe because I have them and I think they work wonders for evenly baking the pastry, but you can, of course, use traditional mini tart pans and pie weights. **MAKES 6 TARTLETS**

To make the pastry: In the bowl of a stand mixer fitted with the paddle attachment, combine 8 tablespoons of the butter with the confectioners' sugar and mix on low until well combined, 1 to 2 minutes. Add one of the egg yolks and continue to mix, stopping to scrape down the sides of the bowl as needed, until everything is thoroughly combined.

Add the salt and flour to the mixer and continue to blend on low until the dough just comes together; you don't want to overwork the dough, so as soon as you can't see any more visible flour, stop the machine and just give it a good knead or two with your hands to bring it all together into a flat round. Cover the dough in plastic wrap and put it in the fridge to chill until it sets up, at least 1 hour. It can also be frozen at this point for up to 3 months.

Preheat the oven to 350°F. Line a baking sheet with parchment paper and clear room in your freezer for it. Set aside.

(recipe continues)

Remove the dough from the fridge, unwrap it, and lay it between two sheets of parchment paper. Working evenly from the center outward, roll the dough into a rectangle about ¼ inch thick. If the dough becomes soft, transfer it, still between the parchment, to the freezer to help it set up again; you want to keep the dough chilled so it can be handled without tearing.

When the dough is an even rectangle, use 4-inch perforated tart rings as cookie cutters and cut out bottoms for each of the six rings. Put the rings, with their dough bottoms in them, on the prepared baking sheet in the freezer to keep them chilled. Then cut long strips from the remaining dough. Remove the rings from the freezer and line the sides of the rings with the strips, pressing gently at the bottom seams to connect the pieces. Once all six rings are completed, trim the tops by running a sharp paring knife along the edge of each ring. Transfer the rings back to the freezer until you're ready to bake.

Place the perforated baking mat directly on the oven rack (no baking sheet) and transfer the chilled tart rings to the mat. Cook for 10 to 12 minutes, until they begin to color on the edges, then remove the rings from the tarts and continue baking for 3 to 5 minutes, until fully set and golden. Remove and let cool completely.

To make the lemon filling: Combine the eggs, the remaining 2 yolks, and granulated sugar in a medium bowl that can be set over a pot of boiling water. Whisk the eggs and sugar until combined, about 1 minute. In a pot slightly smaller than the bowl, bring 2 inches of water to a boil. Place the bowl over the boiling water, reduce the heat to a simmer, and whisk continuously until the sugar begins to dissolve, carefully turning the bowl to make sure it cooks evenly. When the mixture begins to foam, add ¼ cup of the lemon juice and continue whisking. When the mixture thickens, add the remaining ¼ cup lemon juice and whisk until your whisk leaves a trail in the bottom of the pan and the mixture is light yellow. Your total cooking time will be 7 or 8 minutes.

Remove the pot from the heat and whisk in 1 tablespoon of the butter. Add the remaining 3 tablespoons of butter, a tablespoon at a time, until all the butter is incorporated.

Pour the custard into a large glass measuring cup and carefully fill each tart shell to the top. Let sit at room temperature to cool completely and set up fully before serving.

Rhubarb-Plum Cobbler Cake

½ cup (112 grams) unsalted butter, at room temperature, plus more for greasing

1 pound rhubarb, cut into 1-inch pieces

½ pound plums (about 3 medium), halved, pitted, and cut into ½-inch wedges

½ cup (100 grams) granulated sugar, plus 3 tablespoons

3 large eggs

2 teaspoons pure vanilla extract

1 vanilla bean, split lengthwise, seeds scraped and pod discarded (optional)

1 cup (140 grams) all-purpose flour

1 teaspoon baking powder

½ teaspoon sea salt

¼ teaspoon baking soda

3 tablespoons whole milk

1 tablespoon demerara sugar

When you first make this cake, you'll likely wonder how it can possibly work. There isn't a ton of batter and what there is gets spread on the bottom of the pan, then topped with a lot of fruit, so much so that you'll think the fruit will suffocate the batter. It won't. What will happen is the fruit will cook down just enough and the batter will bake up just enough so that you end up with a sponge layer, a moist fruit layer, and, where the fruit and crumb meet, a cobbler-y, crumbly top layer. Sprinkled lightly with demerara sugar for an extra bit of crispness, this is the snacking cake for all of us, those who lean savory and those slain by sweets. SERVES 6 TO 8

Preheat the oven to 375°F. Butter the sides of an 8-inch springform pan. Line the bottom with parchment paper, then butter the parchment.

In a large bowl, combine the rhubarb and plums and sprinkle with 3 tablespoons of the granulated sugar. Toss to coat well and set aside.

In the bowl of a stand mixer fitted with the paddle attachment, beat together ½ cup butter and the remaining ½ cup granulated sugar until pale yellow and quite fluffy, about 5 minutes. Add the eggs, one at a time, mixing well after each addition. Add the vanilla extract and, if using, the vanilla bean seeds. Remove the bowl from the mixer.

In a small bowl, whisk together the flour, baking powder, salt, and baking soda. Use a silicone spatula to fold the flour mixture into the butter-sugar mixture. Add the milk and stir to combine well.

Transfer the batter to the the prepared pan and smooth the top; the batter should come up the sides of the pan only about an inch or so. Spread the fruit on top to completely cover the batter, pressing gently so it is lightly set into the batter.

Put the cake pan on a baking sheet and bake for 20 minutes, then carefully sprinkle with the demerara sugar. Bake for another 20 to 30 minutes, until a skewer inserted into the cake comes out clean and the edges are golden brown. Let the cake cool for 20 minutes before releasing from the pan and transferring to a wire rack to cool completely.

Chapter 9

COUPES, FLUTES, AND JAM JARS

WE'VE MOVED TWICE IN THE PAST FEW YEARS, once from our small city apartment to our weekend cottage and, more recently, to an old house one town over. A lot has changed with this last move, not least of which is we've been embraced by a wealth of friendly neighbors. As people who shared walls with near strangers for years, we now find ourselves in an enclave of interesting and welcoming people. Some stop to chat when they see us out front pulling weeds, some invite us over for spontaneous drinks on the deck, and still others have included us in their seasonal soirees . . . one of those being the Annual Peach Party.

The couple who throw this yearly fête to celebrate the arrival of summer's first peaches go all in with a full bluegrass band, an extravagant peach-based buffet, and, delightfully, a signature peach-centric cocktail—this year it was a peach margarita. While the band was arguably the most spirited part of the party, the cocktail was the most memorable. Not simply because it was a great cocktail (peaches and tequila—what's not to like?) but because there's something about hosts who take the time to devise a single special drink that adds an extra layer of care to a gathering. It's a little thing, but I think it's hugely endearing.

Serving a signature drink when people come over makes an event, intimate or expansive, casual or more refined, feel that much more special. One beverage that departs from the expected, exploits whatever is in season, and makes a bit of a statement is all you need to show your guests you went a little beyond beer and wine.

When we have friends over, the welcoming drinks we make are mixed up small, an amuse-bouche of sorts, something to stir the senses rather than dull them. The sips we like are often topped with bubbles, a bit of Champagne, prosecco, or even soda to add some fizz. They also regularly rely on seasonal ingredients and flavors, subtle twists on the traditional that feel familiar but fresh at the same time. A whiskey smash gets muddled with fresh peach puree, a margarita is brightened with a homemade rhubarb syrup, pomegranate juice is blended with Pimm's. Nothing fancy, but all just a bit fun.

I don't claim to be a mixologist in any way. What I offer in this chapter are a few ideas for relatively simple but still special drinks that we like at our house, each recipe designed to serve four. Take them as is, or use them as starting points and make them your own.

Elderflower and Meyer Lemon 75

2 to 3 cups ice cubes

6 ounces (¾ cup) gin

4 ounces (½ cup)
elderflower liqueur
(such as St-Germain)

2 ounces (¼ cup)
freshly squeezed Meyer
lemon juice (about
2 lemons)

4 ounces (½ cup)
dry bubbles (such as
Champagne, prosecco,
or Cava)

There are cocktails that are meant to blur the harder edges, drinks that almost instantly liberate our inhibitions—a dirty martini or a smoky shot of tequila both come to mind. But then there are drinks that soften and soothe, that slow us down not because of their robust alcohol content but because of their subtle flavors, their seductive ingredients. The French 75 falls into this latter category for me; traditionally a concoction of gin, lemon juice, sugar, and Champagne, here it gets an exotic splash of elderflower in the form of St-Germain, a sexy liqueur that comes in a bottle worthy of expensive perfume, and less acidity courtesy of the Meyer lemon. It's perfect as an aperitif all year-round, but I think it's especially nice at the holidays when the citrus is just coming into season and bubbles abound. If you can't find Meyer lemons, any lemon will work. SERVES 4

In a shaker, shake the ice, gin, elderflower liqueur, and lemon juice to mix well. Strain into coupes, flutes, or whatever glasses you like (including small jam jars), then top with chilled bubbles and serve.

Pomegranate Pimm's Fizz

2 to 3 cups ice cubes

8 ounces (1 cup)
Pimm's No. 1

8 ounces (1 cup)
pomegranate juice

8 ounces (1 cup)
dry bubbles (such
as Champagne,
prosecco, or Cava)

Pomegranate seeds
for garnish (optional)

Pimm's is a British liqueur with a gin base and a vaguely spicy, citrusy flavor. The traditional Pimm's Cup cocktail is made with sparkling lemonade, but I like to mix it with pomegranate juice—because, well, I love pomegranate juice. The puckering sweet-tart of the pomegranate adds just the right amount of fruit and some welcome richness to the Pimm's. It's like a punch without any cloying sweetness. And when topped with Champagne, prosecco, or whatever dry sparkling wine you have, that little bit of effervescence lightens up the whole thing and gives it a fizzy, celebratory feel. If you happen to have pomegranate seeds on hand, drop a few on top just for fun.

SERVES 4

Divide the ice evenly among four tall glasses. Pour 2 ounces (¼ cup) Pimm's and 2 ounces pomegranate juice in each glass and stir to combine. Top each glass with 2 ounces sparkling wine and garnish with a few pomegranate seeds (if using).

Pomegranate Pimm's Fizz (page 239); Elderflower and Meyer Lemon 75 (page 238); Rhubarb Margarita (page 242); and Gruyère Gougères (page 99)

Rhubarb Margarita

2 to 3 cups ice cubes

8 ounces (1 cup) rhubarb syrup (recipe follows)

8 ounces (1 cup) tequila

4 ounces (½ cup) Cointreau

2 ounces (¼ cup) freshly squeezed lime juice

¼ cup kosher salt

1 or 2 blood orange or lime wedges, plus 4 slices for garnish

Besides searching out food markets when I travel, I also try to find local spots where I can buy seeds. Unlike other trinkets, seeds offer a living souvenir of where I've been, a vital and perennial reminder of places and adventures past. I've brought some of the most robust basil seeds home from a stall in the Piazza Navona in Rome, and my rhubarb comes from a packet I picked up in a shop right across from the Seine in Paris. (I've since learned that this is not strictly legal, and I've had to restrain my seed-smuggling tendencies.) These rhubarb plants, which I eagerly await every spring, have had a transient life. They spent their first season in whiskey barrels at our old house, then a few years in a sunny bed in the corner of that garden before being plucked out of the soil when we moved because I couldn't bear to leave them behind. Now they live, happier than ever, in our small vegetable garden between the asparagus (also rather unceremoniously dug up and transplanted in the move) and the strawberry patch we inherited from the previous owners. These plants, a talisman of a trip taken more than a decade ago, remind me both how time has passed and how life continues to flourish. And equally as important, they make a mean margarita. Cooked down into a syrup with a good dose of blood orange, I freeze this blush-toned liquid in ice cube trays, so even post–rhubarb season there's a stash of the tart-sweet syrup that we can use to mix up a pitcher whenever the mood strikes. Beyond the pedigree of the rhubarb, this cocktail isn't reminiscent of France in any way, but it's definitely transporting. **SERVES 4**

Combine the ice, rhubarb syrup, tequila, Cointreau, and lime juice in a shaker. Shake until well chilled. Put the salt in a saucer or small dish. Run a wedge of fruit around the rim of each glass to moisten it and then dip the rim into the salt. Strain the chilled cocktail into the salt-rimmed glasses and garnish with a slice of fruit.

RHUBARB SYRUP

2 pounds rhubarb, chopped (8 cups)   1 cup water

Zest and juice of 1 blood orange   ¼ cup sugar

In a medium saucepan, bring the rhubarb, blood orange zest and juice, and water to a boil. Reduce the heat to a simmer and cook uncovered for 15 to 20 minutes, until the rhubarb has softened and is quite mushy.

Remove from the heat and strain the liquid through a fine-mesh sieve into a medium bowl. Use a silicone spatula or the back of a spoon to press as much liquid as you can out of the fruit. Discard the solids and return the liquid to the saucepan. Add the sugar. Bring the mixture to a boil, then reduce to a simmer, stirring until the sugar is completely dissolved and the syrup is somewhat reduced. Remove from the heat and let cool completely. You should have about 12 ounces (1½ cups) syrup. Store the syrup in an airtight container in the fridge for up to 1 week or pour the syrup into an ice cube tray and freeze for up to 3 months.

Peach Bourbon Blitz

8 ounces (1 cup) peach puree (recipe follows)

4 ounces (½ cup) simple syrup (50/50 blend of water and sugar)

2 ounces (¼ cup) freshly squeezed lemon juice

10 to 12 mint leaves

8 ounces (1 cup) bourbon

2 to 3 cups ice cubes

4 peach slices for garnish

4 mint sprigs for garnish

We are the lucky owners of a very old peach tree. This poor tree is bent and leaning, her trunk half-rotted out and her lower branches stripped clean by the roaming deer. I doubt we'll get many more years out of her, and yet as of now she keeps on trying to give us fruit. It's not a huge bounty, but come August, whatever has survived the birds and worms seems to ripen all at once and we can't possibly eat them all before some start to soften and weep a bit. These are often the sweetest, most honeyed of the lot and they are the ones that I peel, slice, and freeze to use in this cocktail, a variation on the classic Whiskey Smash. When the days start to get shorter and I long for a sip of something redolent of summer, this is the drink that fits my mood. I'm not much of a brown booze person, but there's something about the slightly floral flavor of the peaches, the warming smokiness of the bourbon, and the cool mint that I find hard to resist. SERVES 4

Combine the peach puree, simple syrup, lemon juice, and mint leaves in a pitcher. Using a muddler or the back of a wooden spoon, muddle the mint leaves in the liquid until slightly crushed. Add the bourbon and give it a good stir. Divide first the ice, then the mixture, evenly among four glasses. Garnish each drink with a peach slice and a sprig of mint.

PEACH PUREE
Peel and pit four medium peaches. Transfer the peaches to a blender and puree until smooth, about 1 minute. Strain the mixture through a fine-mesh sieve into a measuring cup. Discard any remaining solids.

Virgin Hibiscus Sunset

2 to 3 cups ice cubes

8 ounces (1 cup)
hibiscus tea
(recipe below)

8 ounces (1 cup)
lemonade
(recipe below)

I can be a bit of a cliché at times. Case in point, as much as the term "sober curious" makes me cringe, I did jump on the no-booze bandwagon for about three months recently. I wasn't doing "dry January" (it was February, and to be a true cliché you have to be a little late to the party), and I didn't have a timeline in mind. One day off just turned into another and then another. And while I didn't crave a drink, I did yearn for something to punctuate the day—a no-booze beverage that at least looked buzzworthy. Starting with the Arnold Palmer as my inspiration, I blended hibiscus tea with lemonade to create a lovely two-toned tipple, one that tastes as heavenly as it looks. Say hello to the Virgin Hibiscus Sunset. SERVES 4

Fill four tall glasses with ice and fill each halfway with lemonade. Using the back of a soup spoon as a guide, slowly pour the hibiscus tea into the glasses, creating two distinct levels of colorful liquid. To enjoy, stir to combine.

HIBISCUS TEA MAKES ABOUT 2 CUPS

2 cups boiling water   ¼ cup dry hibiscus leaves

In a large measuring cup, pour the boiling water over the hibiscus leaves. Let steep for 5 minutes. Strain through a fine-mesh sieve into another measuring cup, discard the leaves, and let the tea cool.

LEMONADE MAKES ABOUT 2 CUPS

6 ounces (¾ cup) freshly squeezed   3 ounces (6 tablespoons) simple
lemon juice   syrup (50/50 blend water and sugar)

6 ounces (¾ cup) water

In a tall glass, stir together the lemon juice, water, and simple syrup to combine.

ACKNOWLEDGMENTS

This book came into being much the way a garden does: A seed (of an idea) grew (slowly and somewhat wildly) before being tended and trimmed. And, like a garden, it benefited from the nurturing hands of more than a few over many seasons.

Erica Clark, thank you again for your taste (both in food and words). Each of these book adventures has been different, but you have been my confidante and confidence booster on all of them.

Andi Delott, the fact that you are now a cook (yes, I take some measure of credit for that) makes me so happy. As does having you as a reader of early drafts and a friend of many decades.

Dervla Kelly, for jumping in with me not once, not twice, but now three times. I can't express how grateful I am to have you as my editor. Not just for the lemons from your garden (for which I am absurdly grateful) but for how completely you got the idea behind this book and how committed you were to bringing it to life.

Kate Jordan, goddess of dappled light, alchemist of connections, and one of the kindest, gentlest humans I know. You brought this book from sapling to soaring; it simply wouldn't be what it is without your collaborative spirit, vision, and generosity.

Christina Lane, thank you for being a bastion of calm and spreader of beauty. And for insisting that one less thing makes everything prettier. When you said yes to this book, the journey became imminently more glorious.

Rae Ann Spitzenberger, I don't know how I got so lucky to work with you again (well, I do—thank you, Dervla and Jenny!). You somehow see what I'm imagining and then make it not just real but a hundred times more gorgeous, more perfect too. I pinch myself that we've gotten to do this together twice.

Jenny Davis, thank you for divining what I was trying to do and working so hard to make it real.

Katherine Leak, Abby Duval, Jennifer Backe, Allison Fox, the folks in marketing and publicity, and the entire Rodale team: Thank you all for being such integral parts of this journey with me.

Angela Miller, as my agent, thank you for your eternal optimism when I call with a new (if long-awaited) idea. And, as my friend, thank you for your ongoing faith that said idea is worth pursuing.

Andie McMahon and Paul Johnson, thanks for being part of this book when it was still just that seed of an idea and for helping it bloom.

Kelly Kubala, having you nearby is always a good thing, especially in the kitchen, especially on this book.

Karen Robbins, thank you for that out-of-the-blue phone call. By supporting my woodworking, you ended up inspiring my book writing. I owe you a bowl.

The writing part of a cookbook is largely solitary, but a lot of the most important work is in the testing and tasting, a process requiring enthusiastic but brutally honest friends. For being game to eat and tell, thank you: Chris, Judy, and Mel Swope; Matt, Roen, and Levi Clark; Kate, Leigh, and Wilder Buckens; Susan Groo; Jeff and Jen Meyer; Ursula Swierczynski; and Stephen Staudigl. And Elana Hershman, for always being there to talk about things other than recipes.

Thank you Ali, Jeremy, and Carolyn—my family—for bearing with all that being related to me entails. And Jackie McCann, while it's a constant frustration that such a big ocean separates us physically, thankfully there's FaceTime so your wit and wisdom never feel quite so far away.

Louise, there's simply not enough space. I hope this works: Thank you.

And Ken. My superpower, my partner in everything. When you weren't at the stove helping me create this book, you were elsewhere in the kitchen, cooking something for us to snack on. I am so lucky.

INDEX

About the Author

Suzanne Lenzer is a food stylist, writer, and the author of *Graze* and *Truly Madly Pizza.* Her styling has appeared in magazines, on television, and in more than two dozen cookbooks, while her writing has been featured in *Tin House* and *The New York Times,* among other publications. Suzanne lives with her husband in Connecticut.